An End to Terrorism

On 20 November 1983, gu... church on Armagh's borde... Republic. They shot three elders and sprayed the congregation with bullets.

Later that evening a former Loyalist paramilitary, Billy McIlwaine, came to the area on a mission of peace.

The deep spiritual experience that drew Billy out of the clutches of violence has been shared by other ex-paramilitaries, both Catholics and Protestants.

What happened to Billy and others gives hope that there is a way out of Northern Ireland's violence and bloodshed.

Peter Jennings was born in London in 1947 and has worked as a freelance journalist since the early 1970s, writing chiefly about religious and Irish affairs. A Catholic, he is actively committed to the cause of Christian unity. His wife, Stella, is an evangelical Anglican. Their daughter Sarah was born in April 1983.

An end to TERRORISM

Peter Jennings

A LION PAPERBACK
Tring · Belleville · Sydney

Copyright © 1984 Peter Jennings

Published by
Lion Publishing plc
Icknield Way, Tring, Herts, England
ISBN 0 85648 648 5
Albatross Books
PO Box 320, Sutherland, NSW 2232, Australia
ISBN 0 86760 601 0

First edition 1984
All rights reserved

Phototypeset by Gecko Limited, Bicester
Printed and bound in Great Britain by
Cox and Wyman Ltd, Reading

*This book is dedicated to everyone
who is working for peace and reconciliation
in Northern Ireland.*

Foreword

This has been one of the most exciting projects it has been my privilege to be involved in. I have written about Irish affairs for many years, but never before have I been so encouraged by anything that has happened in Northern Ireland. Is God bringing his own answer to the seemingly endless troubles? Men and women from both sides of the religious divide who were once at the heart of the sectarian violence are being changed through genuine response to Jesus Christ. They are now working for peace and reconciliation among their former paramilitary colleagues.

This book would not have been possible without the continuous help and co-operation given to me over many months by ex-Loyalist paramilitary Billy McIlwaine and his wife, Sally. Not only have they lived through the traumatic events of this book, but they have re-lived them for me, sometimes at great personal cost. Their patient forbearance has often been tried, but they never lost confidence in the project.

I am deeply indebted to Mary Smyth, an ex-Republican paramilitary, who has allowed me the privilege of including her story. The debt extends also to ex-Loyalist paramilitaries Jackie Gourley and Kenny McClinton, and to housewife Mrs Florence Cobb whose life demonstrates the power of forgiveness.

My thanks for help given also go to Sally Bufton, Mary Bunter, Ann Evans, Steve Goddard and Patrick

Hennessy. Reports in *The Irish Times* have been a constant source of help as background to some of the events included in the book.

Finally I should like to express my heartfelt love to my wife, Stella. Her continual encouragement and support have helped me throughout the writing of this book.

Birmingham,
August 1984

Contents

Introduction
The Background to the Troubles

In 1920 the Government of Ireland Act was passed which allowed for two parliaments, one for the twenty-six counties of Southern Ireland and one for the six counties of Northern Ireland. The Irish Republican Army (IRA) waged a guerrilla campaign to secure the severance of links between Britain and Ireland. In December 1921 a Treaty was concluded between Lloyd George's Coalition Government and the Southern Ireland Parliament, by which the Irish Free State came into being as a self-governing state outside the United Kingdom.

The Treaty caused a division both in Sinn Fein, a nationalist party founded in 1905, and in the IRA. In 1926 the faction of Sinn Fein led by Eamon de Valera who had opposed the Treaty decided to recognize the Southern Irish Parliament.

In 1949 Southern Ireland became a republic. The Ireland Act 1949 passed by the United Kingdom Parliament recognized its status as an independent republic. The Act also contained a declaration that Northern Ireland remained part of the United Kingdom and that it would not cease to be so without the consent of the Northern Ireland Parliament.

The 1920 Government of Ireland Act was unacceptable to many members of the Catholic minority in the North and partition became the principle issue in Northern Ireland politics. With the largely Protestant majority of voters in favour of continuing union with the United

Kingdom, every general election gave a majority to the Unionist Party. Unionists believed that a United Ireland would lead not only to a reduced standard of living but also to a loss of Protestant identity in a society with a different religious and cultural tradition. At the same time the Catholic community in the North resented the continuing domination of what it regarded as a hostile government. Up to 1969, every member of the Northern Ireland Cabinet was a Protestant and a member of the Unionist Party.

In the late 1960s an active and articulate civil rights movement emerged which sought to achieve electoral reform, the ending of discrimination against Catholics in employment and housing, and the disbanding of the 'B Specials' – an armed part-time force which helped the police with security duties. The principal supporters of the civil rights movement were in favour of change through non-violent means when the first civil rights march took place on 24 August 1968 from Coalisland to Dungannon.

The following year serious rioting broke out in Derry and Belfast. Petrol bombs were used against the police who responded with CS gas to disperse the crowds during the 'Battle of the Bogside'. Two days later on 14 August 1969 the British Army was sent onto the streets of Derry as the trouble rapidly spread throughout Northern Ireland.

The situation became progressively worse and on 24 March 1972 the Northern Ireland Parliament, which sat at Stormont, near Belfast, was suspended and direct rule of the Province began from Westminster.

The campaign of violence and terrorism by the Provisional IRA, Irish National Liberation Army, and such Loyalist paramilitary organizations as the Ulster Volunteer Force, has continued unabated year after year. Between 1 January 1969 and 30 June 1984, 2,387 people had lost their lives in Northern Ireland as a result of the troubles.

MAPS

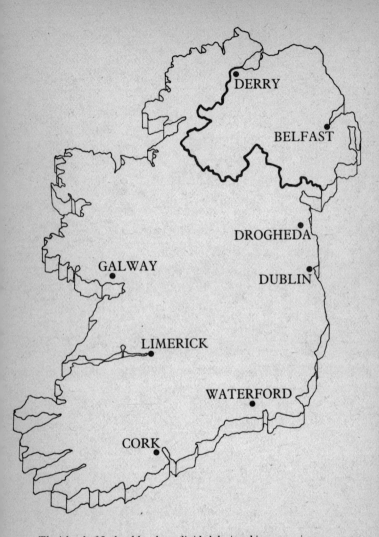

The island of Ireland has been divided during this century into two parts, under quite different systems of government. The twenty-six counties south of the border form an independent republic, a member-state of the European Community. The six counties north of it are part of the United Kingdom. Nationalists long for a united Ireland; Unionists are determined that the 256-mile-long border shall stay.

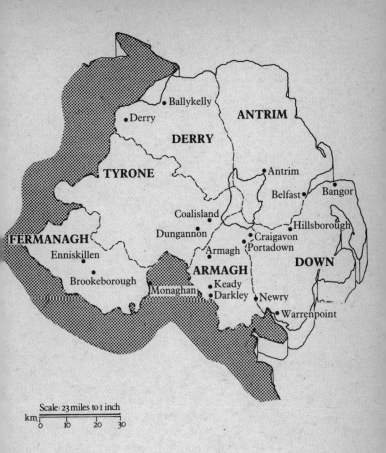

Northern Ireland comprises six of the nine counties of the ancient Irish province of Ulster: Antrim, Armagh, Down, Fermanagh, Londonderry and Tyrone. It has a population of just under 1,600,000 people. Its area is 5,542 square miles, about the size of Yorkshire. At one point it is separated from Scotland by only thirteen miles of sea.

1

Massacre at Mountain Lodge

On Sunday, 20 November 1983, gunmen burst into a Pentecostal meeting hall near Darkley, on the Armagh-Monaghan border in Northern Ireland, killing three church elders in the hallway and spraying the congregation with bullets.

Inside the small, isolated Mountain Lodge Pentecostal church a congregation of more than sixty people had just started to sing a hymn while waiting for the evening service to begin. Suddenly, without any warning, came the sound of gunfire. Arriving at the porch of the wooden building under cover of darkness two gunmen opened fire with automatic weapons at point-blank range. In the porch the three church elders, Harold Brown, Victor Cunningham and David Wilson, had been welcoming members of the congregation. Two of them died instantly.

Amid screams of terror, the third man, David Wilson, fatally wounded and with blood pouring from his face, staggered into the church shouting 'Get down'. The congregation dived for cover behind the wooden pews as the injured man struggled on towards the back door where he fell dead in an ante-room behind the pulpit.

The gunmen then turned their weapons on the helpless congregation and opened fire indiscriminately. Men, women and children screamed hysterically as they lay on the floor among the scattered hymn-books and Bibles.

The gunmen then calmly reloaded and, as they made their escape, sprayed the thin exterior wall of the pre-fabricated building with another hail of bullets. They fled in a waiting car for the border with the Irish Republic, a little more than a mile away. Inside the church three men lay dead and seven people injured, some seriously.

A group calling itself the Catholic Reaction Force claimed responsibility for the massacre. It was alleged that this was just a cover name for INLA – the Irish National Liberation Army.

The terrorists struck as the congregation were singing a song popular with Pentecostals:

Have you been to Jesus for the cleansing Power?
Are you washed in the blood of the Lamb?

The wooden double doors through which the gunmen had first fired were pierced by nine bullet holes. The walls, windows and ceiling were riddled with more than thirty more as a result of the random firing. None of those killed or injured had any connection with the security forces in Northern Ireland, nor was the Gospel Hall ever attended by members of the security forces. On that particular Sunday evening those present included more than twenty-four children under the age of fourteen.

Painted brown, with a green roof, Mountain Lodge church stands on a desolate hillside some distance from Darkley in the heart of the notorious Republican 'bandit country' of South Armagh. The rugged, mountainous terrain and narrow, winding lanes made it easy for the gunmen to escape. In the porch was a poster inscribed with the 'The Ten Fundamentals of Faith'. The last of them read: 'That every believer should exhibit holiness and charity in life and conduct, and actively witness for the Lord as opportunities permit.' Members of the congregation were to show ample evidence of this Christian fundamental in the days that followed.

Pastor Robert Bain was just about to start his service when the first gunshots rang out from the back of the Gospel Hall. Later the fifty-eight-year-old pastor described the scene of horror he had looked on as he crouched behind his pulpit:

> The shooting began at about 6.15 p.m. when the congregation were singing hymns and choruses before the start of the service proper at 6.30. I was on the platform with my son, Bobbie, who led a few choruses and then handed over to me. I dived down behind the pulpit. One of the elders who'd been shot rushed up the aisle and out through the ante-room. I saw him lying dead. My daughter, who was in the congregation, was shot in the elbow. A young man was badly wounded in the stomach. His wife was shot in the back. They were bleeding badly. Children were crying. If the gunmen had come into the service many more people would have been shot. I went into the hallway. One man was lying dead on top of the other. Harold Brown was lying with his face towards the door.

Pastor Bain repeatedly said that he wanted no reprisals for the killings. He was praying for the gunmen who had brought such devastation to his Gospel Hall.

2

What Possible Good?

That evening, as the shock waves echoed around Northern Ireland, Billy McIlwaine drove to Armagh to visit distraught members of the congregation. Billy was once a member of a Loyalist paramilitary organization, but this time he was on a mission of peace and reconciliation. On 24 July 1979 he had become a committed Christian.

On the day of the Darkley killings Billy had attended the morning service at his own Assembly in Belfast. Towards the end of the meetings there anyone in the fellowship is free to take part. That day he felt the Lord prompting him to speak about Stephen the deacon who was stoned to death.

> I spoke about how in the Bible Saul of Tarsus, a persecutor of Christians, had stood by and watched while Stephen was being stoned to death. I mentioned how Ananias had been told by God in a vision to go and lay hands on Saul. At the time he didn't know that Saul had been converted on the road to Damascus. I asked the congregation how many of them would go to Gerry Adams, the President of Sinn Fein, the political wing of the Provisional IRA, and lay hands on him and pray for him if the Lord told them to do so. I said the Lord showed me that what we need in Northern Ireland is a forgiving and loving spirit, in order to conquer the evil that is in the land.

On Sunday evening Billy had just arrived home when he heard the news about the Darkley killings on the radio. He had been to a service in the Methodist church in the Shankhill Road, where he shared what he had said in the morning. He tried to telephone a friend of his, Jimmy, who lives just outside Armagh, but his telephone was engaged for a long time. When Billy finally got through his friend was crying.

Jimmy had been in the Mountain Lodge church with his wife and two young children. He also had a dozen kids from Armagh City whom he picked up in a minibus and brought to the service each week so that they too could hear the good news about Jesus. They were sitting towards the front of the building and his wife and children were near the back. Most of the gunfire had been aimed at the back and it was a miracle that none of his family were injured because the wooden pews were riddled with bullets.

Billy was numb when he left Belfast at about 9.30 p.m. Jackie Gourley, another former Loyalist paramilitary now a Christian, was with him. He too felt numb. Billy knew the great danger of what this numbness could turn to; how they could begin to think about retaliation for what had happened at Darkley. He reminded Jackie and himself that they were Christians now and should not think along those evil lines. On the way to Armagh Billy stopped at Portadown to see a young former Loyalist paramilitary who had only recently become a Christian. He was afraid for him in case he was thinking about retaliation, but was encouraged to find that this had not even entered his friend's thoughts.

Billy was expecting to find all kinds of security precautions in force on the way, but there was not one road block even in the Armagh area. When he arrived Jimmy was still crying. Billy tried to get across to him that God had in no way lost control. He was praying inwardly all the time that he would be effective in what he said. Everyone in the house was in a state of deep shock and any wild talk about retaliation could have had disastrous consequences. Later Billy said:

I believe that it was God's will that the three men who were killed should die as a testimony. I believe that the angels of the Lord were protecting that congregation. Sometimes it is very hard to put into words why God allows certain things to happen. God is supremely sovereign and we cannot question his ways.

In the fourteen-year campaign of terrorism in Northern Ireland no incident before the Darkley killings had involved cold-blooded murder of people at worship. The Province reached a new low on 20 November 1983. There was a deep and widespread reaction in Ireland and beyond.

A rare statement was put out, signed by the leaders of the four main churches in Ireland, Catholic, Church of Ireland, Presbyterian and Methodist:

This act of sectarian slaughter, directed indiscriminately against a worshipping community, goes beyond anything hitherto perpetrated. It seems to be a calculated effort to provoke further community strife in Co Armagh and elsewhere. Those who are guilty of such infamous deeds have rejected the Gospel of Jesus Christ.

These leaders visited the three widows to express their sympathy. After a visit to the Cunningham home about four miles from Armagh, Cardinal O Fiaich, Catholic Archbishop of Armagh and Primate of All Ireland, said that he was deeply impressed by the faith, courage, resignation and sense of forgiveness which he had found in the home.

In an earlier statement he had made it clear that to do this thing when people were at prayer in their local place of worship added the guilt of sacrilege and blasphemy to that of murder. To those responsible he said, 'Don't dare to claim the name Catholic for your band of evil-doers'.

The Church of Ireland Primate, Archbishop Armstrong said:

> Those who in any way support the perpetrators of these and other murders are no less guilty than the killers themselves. I call upon all Church of Ireland people to exercise restraint in words and actions at this critical moment.

Irish Prime Minister Dr Garret FitzGerald gave a BBC interview the day after the killings:

> It's an appalling event which should show anyone where violence leads. The people who think they're carrying on a war of liberation are bringing all Ireland down in anarchy.
>
> In Ireland there really are only two kinds of people. It's not Catholic and Protestant or Nationalist and Unionist; it's those who are prepared to use violence to achieve their aims, and the rest of us who want to live in peace together and to work towards legitimate political objectives by peaceful means only, and who will stand against violence no matter what the cost or what the circumstances.

The Irish Times made a significant point in an editorial:

> The Darkley slaughter will dismay some of those in the South who claim that Republicans do not murder Protestants *as* Protestants. Protestants are murdered, it is said, because they are in the security forces. This has been disproved by Sunday's incident.

In their next day's editorial this paper saw a ray of hope:

> There is no easy or quick way in which the Christian message can bring peace to this troubled area, but there is a firm base for mutual regard when the spiritual leaders show such solidarity and compassion. This dreadful massacre may remind both sides how much they have in common, how much, in the end, they depend on each other.

A few days later they came back to this subject:

> The unusual aspect of the recent slaughter has been the devastating candour and forgiveness on the part of the Pentecostalists. It has been startling, almost shocking, as such naked appeals to basic Christianity tend to be. No reproach; no hatred; indeed an appeal to the gunmen to come and be forgiven.
>
> It is good that some today can still see man as never beyond reform and redemption. We need that in this blackest month, which in the Christian calendar should be the month of reawakening hope.

The Times of London had a poignant back-page feature, 'Divided by time, united by violence and grief:'

> Two families, an ocean apart, paying tribute to their lost loved ones: two men who had died by the gun.
>
> Twenty years ago, President John Fitzgerald Kennedy was shot dead as he drove through Dallas, Texas. Two days ago, Mr Victor Cunningham was murdered as he worshipped in a Pentecostal hall in Co Armagh. Two others died with him. Yesterday prayers were offered for both men.
>
> In Arlington, Virginia, the President's only surviving brother Edward spoke the eulogy at a memorial service to mark the anniversary of the assassination. In Armagh, Mrs Edna Cunningham said her last farewell to her husband.

The bereaved spoke words of forgiveness. Elizabeth Wilson, the sister of one of the victims, appealed for no reprisals. She sobbed at the doorway of his home as she said, 'Let there be no tit-for-tat killings. In God's name, let there be no reprisals'.

Mrs Elizabeth Brown took the same approach:

> What use are words? The Lord giveth, and the Lord taketh away. We have no hate at all and have forgiven the terrorists.

Harold Brown was one of the founders of the little church.

The singing of gospel hymns was only interrupted by the clatter of an army helicopter overhead and rooks in the tall copper beeches of the country churchyard. This was the funeral of Victor Cunningham, the first of the three Mountain Lodge massacre victims to be buried.

The singing brought back horrific memories for those who had been in the church on Sunday night. Then the joyful chorus had been transformed to screeches of terror as the shots rang out in the hallway of the wooden church.

Pastor Bain told several hundred mourners at the graveside: 'Victor is better off than his killers; he's in the presence of the Lord whom he loved.'

The dead man's mother, supported at the graveside by her family, broke down and had to be comforted. His widow Edna closed her eyes and raised her hands to heaven, her wedding ring glinting in the dying winter sun. 'In the sweet by-and-by we shall meet on that beautiful shore,' she sang with the rest.

In Armaghbreague churchyard the following day, Pastor Bain said:

I've never had such a burden on my heart like I had on Sunday night and I never felt such a great flow of the Spirit as after it – out of this tragedy people are coming to know God.

In a home last night I heard from a young woman that when the tape of hymn-singing was played on the radio with the burst of gunfire that riddled the place in the middle of the last verse, five young people who were listening fell down on their knees and accepted Jesus Christ as their own personal Saviour.

In an interview for the BBC Radio 4 programme *Sunday*, Pastor Bain said:

We can't close shop because three of our main men were mowed down. I believe that out of this tragedy God is going to do a work in people's hearts round the country. We are going on.

In an interview broadcast on the same programme Mrs Elizabeth Brown said:

I want to say to every home in Northern Ireland and down South that we want no retaliation whatsoever for what has happened. Our best friends were Catholics. We prayed together and talked about Jesus, many a time to the early hours of the morning.

After doing what he could to help, Billy left Jimmy's home in Armagh at about 1.15 a.m. on Monday morning and was not stopped once by the security forces on his way back home to Belfast. In the morning he telephoned Jimmy to see how he was and found him still very shocked.

On Tuesday morning Billy took three white floral crosses to the homes of the three widows. They were from the 'Soldiers of the Cross', a fellowship for ex-paramilitaries who had become Christians. He said prayers with Mrs Cunningham and in the afternoon went to her husband's funeral, which he described as 'a service of victory'.

He then visited the homes of the other two victims where he also said a prayer before he went with some other people to visit the church. They felt a bit apprehensive because they had not seen one army or police patrol all night. They went into the Mountain Lodge Pentecostal church and put the lights on. There was still a great deal of blood on the floor. They decided to pray outside the church and claim the victory in the name of Jesus. They asked the Lord to bring the men who had committed this foul deed to repentance. They also asked him to put his protecting hand on the little church.

The next afternoon Billy drove to Craigavon Hospital to see the victims who had been injured in the shooting. One girl had had an operation to remove a bullet from her nose. Her boyfriend had been shot in the thigh as they were singing. There was no talk of hatred or retaliation among any of the people who had been injured. One girl turned to Billy and said, 'I forgive those who have attacked me'.

Billy went back to Armagh and attended the funerals of the other two victims. He also planned to take members of the Soldiers of the Cross to the Mountain Lodge church on Sunday and hold services of praise and thanksgiving.

> I told Pastor Bain that members of the Soldiers of the Cross were willing to defy the gunmen on the border not with guns but with the Bible. I did not want to see the flame of the gospel extinguished in the border area.

For various reasons the church remained closed on the Sunday following the killings.

On 24 November I went with Billy to Armagh. Together with Jimmy and his wife we drove to the Gospel Hall which I had never heard of before the previous Sunday evening. I felt a strange coldness all over me as we entered. The bullet holes had white chalk rings round them. There was dried blood on the scattered hymn-books and Bibles, as well as on the floor. Some cleaning up had been done and that particular afternoon men from the congregation had brought tins of plastic wood to fill in the holes left by the bullets. We all stood for a few minutes in a circle and held hands while I prayed that great goodness would come out of this evil that had been done. As Billy and I left, a late November mist added to the bleakness of an area which had suffered many sectarian killings.

Billy reminded me of the pattern of sectarian killing in the area. In September 1975, six Protestants were shot dead in nearby Tullyvallen Orange Hall by the Provisional IRA, using the cover name 'Republican Action Force'. On 4 January 1976, five Catholics were shot dead in two attacks by a Loyalist paramilitary organization calling itself 'Protestant Action Force'. The following day ten Protestant workers were taken off a bus at Kingsmills about fifteen miles from Darkley and machine-gunned to death by the Provisional IRA.

Cold-blooded terrorist murder in Northern Ireland has now become such a frequent occurrence that it often rates no more than a paragraph or two tucked away on the inside pages of the newspapers. The Darkley killings were different. They brought condemnation from all shades of political opinion. *The bells did not toll for Daniel Rouse* was a headline in *The Irish Times* on 28 November 1983. The report said:

> No passing bells for the funeral of Daniel Rouse, beaten to death at one in the morning as he walked home after

having a drink. No television cameras, no big political names among the mourners, and very few reporters. And yet Mr Rouse was as vulnerable a target as the worshippers at Darkley, and as innocent, and he died because they did.

Mr Rouse was fifty-one, a Catholic from Meadow-brook Estate in Craigavon. He left a widow and three children. Mass in St Anthony's, a new church in the middle of rundown and semi-derelict Craigavon, was crowded. But the noon Mass always is.

3

Billy McIlwaine

Billy McIlwaine was born on 10 March 1943 at 98 Wilton Street, off the Shankill Road in Belfast. He was christened William Henry at St Luke's Church of Ireland in Northumberland Street. His father, also called William, worked as a labourer in Short Brothers Aircraft factory. He died in 1961. His mother, Annie, died in 1974. Billy had five brothers and five sisters, and the family home – no bathroom and only two bedrooms – was far too small for them. They were poor, and the children depended largely on other families for second-hand clothes and shoes.

The Shankill Road where the McIlwaine family lived is among the oldest in Belfast. Originally it was a track from the old church to the crossing of the River Lagan. The name Shankill is a derivation of the old Gaelic words *sean cill*, 'old church'. Earliest maps show it as the 'Antrim Road', passing westwards from the town centre up over Peter's Hill and through open countryside to Ligoniel and beyond. The development of the Shankill in the mid nineteenth century was due largely to the growth of the linen industry in Belfast. Socially the Shankill has always been working-class; politically strongly Unionist.

From 1948 until 1954, Billy went to St Saviours Primary school in Southland Street. At the age of nine he was knocked down by a car which mounted the pavement and hit him on the back as he was going to a football match one Saturday morning. He was at first temporarily paralyzed and later affected by a feeling of choking and not being able to breathe. His mother took him to all kinds of doctors but to no avail, and the accident affected his nervous system for some years afterwards.

Billy's first impression of the Irish Republic came from his mother. She told him about the smuggling of nylon stockings, butter and cigarettes from across the border where everything was cheaper than it was in Belfast.

In 1954, through the influence of his older sister Ella, Billy became a committed Christian. She took him to the Church of God in Craven Street and he accepted Jesus to be the Saviour of his life.

At the age of eleven Billy transferred to Everton Secondary school in the Crumlin Road. Some of his schoolfriends were also Christians and they all attended a Pentecostal church on the Shankill Road. Billy and three friends usually had to sit at the side of the platform because the hall was full of adults. Often they were asked to lead the singing. He still remembers the all-night prayer meetings and the lively singing of gospel songs. They held open-air services on the Shankill Road and were much encouraged when people came to be personally committed to Jesus after hearing them speak.

In 1956 at a gospel service in the YMCA's Wellington Hall in Belfast, an American evangelist, Jack Coe, prayed specifically that Billy's right ear, which had been giving him severe trouble since birth, would be healed. He received healing and has not had any trouble with his ear since.

Billy joined the Boy Scouts, but along with the normal activities he spent a lot of time praying and reading and studying the Bible. He would go to the scoutmaster's flat at the weekend and pray all through the night. When he was thirteen, Billy was given the opportunity to preach in Belfast. In 1959, at the age of sixteen, Billy was invited by a Belfast preacher to go and study at a Bible School in the United States. But he did not go. This was because he had become disillusioned by some Christians whom he thought were not behaving and acting as they should. It became a major distraction to him:

> I started to judge people. I backslid because I looked at the faults and shortcomings of older Christians and gradually I stopped going to church and reading my Bible.

Billy lied about his age and joined The Royal Ulster Rifles, an infantry battalion of the Territorial Army, at Victoria Barracks in Belfast. His brother Charlie had told him about the weekend camps. He was also attracted by the money, the trips, the uniforms and the good nightlife. He started drinking cheap wine and beer. Why?

'I drank because it gave me false courage when I went to dances,' he says. 'It also made me feel I was big in stature as a person.'

Billy joined the British Army on 13 April 1961 at Clifton Street in Belfast. His regiment was The Royal Army Service Corps (RASC) which later became The Royal Corps of Transport. His first impression of army life was terrible. He arrived at the Aldershot Training Depot and hated it. It was the first time he had been in England.

I wrote home and asked my mother to buy me out of the Army but she hadn't got the money so there was nothing for me to do but make the best of a bad decision.

Billy stayed at Aldershot for three months doing square-bashing, arms training and other basic soldiering. He became interested in long-distance running and was picked to run for the training battalion. He was then sent to Yeovil in Somerset for driver training. He enjoyed the atmosphere which was a lot more relaxed. He failed his driving test twice but finally passed at the third attempt.

After three months' training in Yeovil Billy went home on leave. To spend more time with his girl-friend he sent a doctor's certificate. By the time he got back to the depot all his friends had their postings and had gone to their various battalions in Aden, Singapore, Germany and East Africa. Billy, unlike the rest of the lads, now had no choice. The only posting available was Kenya. He left England in the latter part of 1961.

When he first arrived in Kenya Billy felt something of a prisoner knowing that he could not leave for at least three years whether he liked the place or not. He was sent first to Gil Gil, a little village about sixty miles from Nairobi. He was part of an RASC company in which about a hundred men did all kinds of transport duties throughout Kenya. He did not like the camp which was isolated, regimented and mucky during the rainy season. Soon he was given a new base in a field ambulance a few miles outside Nairobi. In the new camp he was working with army doctors and medical personnel and the regime was not nearly so strict. Billy met up with other drivers:

Our greatest common denominator was the booze which we all loved very dearly. We were in the NAAFI drinking at every chance we got. We formed an association called the Alsops Alcoholics Association. Alsops was our favourite brand of beer.

They also carried hip flasks about with them to make sure they were never too far away from the booze.

The drink landed Billy and his friends in trouble many times. His wild living earned Billy many short periods in military prison and he was recommended for court martial.

Billy enjoyed his three years in Kenya but he was glad when August 1964 arrived and it was time to go back home to Northern Ireland. He was met at the dock by some of his brothers and sisters who took him by 'black taxi' to the Shankill Road.

I remember going into the house and throwing my arms around my mother whom I had missed so much. It was great to be home with the neighbours coming in and out to see Annie McIlwaine's wee son who had been away in the wilds of Africa.

After some leave Billy was posted to the British Army Northern Ireland Headquarters at Lisburn outside Belfast. It was a boring life driving army lorries around Northern Ireland. After he had been there for about a year it was discovered that he had duodenal ulcers. On 1 February 1966, he was given a medical discharge and an army pension.

During his time in Kenya Billy's sister Margaret, who lived in the United States, wrote and asked if he would like to write to her friend Sally McClure. Billy became a very dedicated pen-friend to Sally and looked forward to her letters about herself and her family. In July 1965 Margaret and Sally came to Northern Ireland on a three-week holiday, and Billy started taking Sally out.

Their first date was at a dance in Bangor, Co Down. Billy really enjoyed himself and knew that he would take Sally out on more dates. During the short time she was at home their relationship deepened and Billy went to meet her mother and father who lived in Ivan Street in the York Road area of Belfast. They were both twenty-three years old when Billy asked Sally to marry him before she returned to her job in America. After his medical discharge from the Army Billy changed his mind about going to join Sally in America. He wrote and asked her to come back to Belfast to marry him. Sally arrived on Christmas Eve 1965 and they became engaged that day.

Billy and Sally were married on 17 September 1966 in North Belfast City Mission in York Street in the docks area of Belfast. They spent their honeymoon in a caravan lent to them by one of Billy's sisters. They put all their savings into their first home which was in Craigs Terrace off the Shankill Road. Their only daughter, Rhonda, was born on 5 November 1968 in the Royal Victoria Hospital in Belfast.

The following year violence erupted on the streets of Belfast and Derry and life for Billy and Sally would never be quite the same again.

4
The Troubles

Serious trouble erupted in Belfast during 1969 between Catholics and Protestants from the Falls Road, Springfield Road, Ardoyne and Shankill Road. From the time of his discharge from the Army, Billy had been working as a lathe operator in James Mackie's Iron Foundry on the Springfield Road. Once things got out of hand he was rarely at work. He was on the streets most nights helping to defend areas of Shankill Road that would be vulnerable to attack from Republicans.

I remember the panic there was in my area as I lay down for a short nap after dinner one evening. My wife began shaking me furiously saying, 'The Catholics are coming up from the Falls Road to attack us!' That was the start of several nights of serious violence in Belfast during which people on both sides lost their lives.

Billy had never known what Molotov cocktails (petrol bombs) were made of. He had only ever seen them when they were shown on the television news in major disturbances in cities throughout the world. When he arrived in Percy Street, which runs from the Shankill Road to the Falls Road, a battle was raging. Petrol bombs, bottles, bricks and large pieces of concrete and metal were being used as ammunition. A lot of people were using bin lids as cover for their bodies against the barrage of oncoming missiles. A barricade had been erected across the street separating the two factions. The Catholics had a bulldozer on their side of the barricade. During the night the bulldozer was hit by a petrol bomb and the driver had to jump for his life.

A car stopped Billy in Northumberland Street and the driver asked him where he could get through the rioting to a local hospital. He had a woman in the car who had gunshot wounds in the back.

'I realized then,' says Billy, 'that guns were being used in the streets which I had known since I was a child.'

The battle raged one way and then the other. For a time the Catholics would have the Protestants on the run, then it would suddenly change and the Catholics would retreat. There was no real police presence as the Royal Ulster Constabulary had mostly been drafted out to try and contain the riots which had started in Derry before they spread to Belfast.

After some hours Billy left the Percy Street area and went further up the Shankill Road to see what was happening. A lot of Catholic homes were burning and it looked to him as though the Protestants had broken through almost onto the Falls Road itself. A Catholic bar had been looted and people were sitting around the back entries drinking the remains of the contents. After a short time there Billy decided to go back down to his own part of the Shankill Road.

As he got nearer to home he could hear the sound of gunfire very clearly. He made his way very slowly, under cover of the darkness, crawling from hallway to hallway. After reassuring his wife that there was no threat to her and their baby daughter, he went back towards the Falls Road again to see what the situation was like. A sniper was firing from the top of Divis Flats in the Lower Falls at anything that moved in the Percy

Street area. It was very difficult to get from one side of the street to the other without being raked by a hail of bullets. RUC marksmen had been summoned to flush out the gunman. There was distant shooting through-out the night but Billy decided to stay nearer home as he felt there would be no further threat to his area that particular night.

A short time after the outbreak of violence Billy left his job and decided to become a full-time paid member of a Loyalist paramilitary organization. This was to be his way of life for the next ten years. His responsibility was 'to raise finances for the day-to-day running of the organization'. As a Protestant Billy feared a United Ireland under a Dublin government, and he was pre-pared to take up the gun to make sure that it did not happen.

On 11 December 1971 there was a huge explosion in a furniture showroom on the Shankill Road. A 'no-warn-ing' bomb planted by the Provisional IRA killed four people. Billy was in a nearby bar when he heard the blast. He ran to the scene.

There was a lot of panic. People were screaming. I remember a mother crying for her baby. We started digging frantically at the rubble with our bare hands but we didn't make much headway until an army bulldozer arrived. I will never forget seeing a little child's leg being ripped up as the mechanical shovel clawed away at the rubble.

Sickened, Billy left the scene and returned to the bar. He found it very hard to accept little children being kil-led during the campaign of violence.

In the early 1970s some of Billy's close friends were assassinated or met violent deaths. One friend and colleague blew himself to death while making a bomb intended for use against the Provisional IRA. During this time Billy depended more and more on alcohol to give him some kind of solace.

At the end of an anti-internment rally in the Bogside area of Derry on 30 January 1972, some of the large crowd started to throw stones at the British troops. At first the troops responded with rubber bullets, water cannons and CS gas. Shots were fired by the Paratroopers and in minutes thirteen civilians lay dead in and around the courtyard of the Rossville Flats. A young priest, Father Edward Daly, waved a white handkerchief while administering the last rites to a dying victim on what has become known as 'Bloody Sunday'. Today that priest is Bishop of Derry and a photograph of one young victim is still beside his study desk. He told me:

> Hatred spews from those who have suffered least. I have picked up pieces of human body and I am always amazed at the ability of people to forgive. Both communities in Northern Ireland have suffered a tremendous amount over the years but there is no difference between the tears of grief shed by a Catholic or a Protestant.

On 'Bloody Sunday', Billy was at home in Belfast when he heard on the television news that people had been shot dead by the Army in Derry. 'I was really glad that the Army was starting to sort out the Provisional IRA.'

Already the UDA (Ulster Defence Association) had been formed, as it claimed, 'to defend the citizens of Ulster against the armed aggression of the Provisional IRA'.

On 18 March 1972, during a huge Protestant rally in Ormeau Park in Belfast, William Craig, MP, made a speech:

> We must build up a dossier of the men and women who are a menace to this country because it may be our job to liquidate the enemy.

Incitement from speeches like these, made by various Loyalist politicians, encouraged young men to join paramilitary organizations.

The Northern Ireland Parliament at Stormont was suspended by the British Government on 20 March 1972. Direct rule of the Province from Westminster began. William Whitelaw, now Viscount Whitelaw, was appointed as the first Secretary of State for Northern Ireland by Prime Minister Edward Heath.

> I don't believe that a security initiative on its own will ever finally succeed in Northern Ireland. An army can subdue a guerrilla movement so that they lose a great deal of their effectiveness and initiative, but an army cannot actually win in that sense. I cannot envisage a time of complete withdrawal of the British Army and I believe that any premature withdrawal could lead to a very nasty situation. Northern Ireland is part of the United Kingdom and therefore the protection of its citizens is the responsibility of the British Government.

He reflected on his controversial face-to-face negotiations with leaders of the Provisional IRA in London on 7 July 1972:

> Once the British Government had talked and had exposed the total absence of any real feeling on the part of the Provisional IRA to stop violence, a lot of Catholics began to see that I was acting in good faith and that the IRA were not

and withdrew their support from them. It could be argued that the way was then cleared for the removal of the 'no-go' areas by the Motorman Operation.

In this operation on 31 July 1972, the British Army entered the 'no-go' areas of West Belfast and the Bogside in Derry.

Billy recalls that time. He remembers that there was not much opposition to the Army from the Loyalists. To a certain degree, they were happy to see the Army removing the barricades in their areas because they knew that exactly the same would have to happen in the Catholic areas. Then the Army could go in and search for the gunmen.

William Whitelaw was replaced by Francis Pym on 2 December 1973, a few days before the tripartite London-Belfast-Dublin talks at Sunningdale, which led to the establishment of the short-lived Power-Sharing Executive in Northern Ireland. In February the following year Labour won the British General Election, called as a result of the miners' strike and the three-day working week in Britain. Merlyn Rees was appointed Secretary of State for Northern Ireland. On 14 May the Loyalist Workers' Council called a general strike throughout Northern Ireland. The Province was brought to a standstill and the Power-Sharing Executive collapsed.

On 15 August 1975 Billy was caught in a bomb explosion in which five people were killed by the Provisional IRA. He was in the lounge of the Bayardo bar on the Shankill Road, having a drink with a colleague, when they heard gunfire. They started to make a run for it when a bomb was tossed in the front door and a bomb in a duffle bag thrown in the side door. At the same time the bar was raked with armalite gunfire. Billy remembers seeing an almighty flash in front of his eyes. The next thing he knew he was being buried beneath the rubble from the upstairs of the bar. The force of the blast ripped the only suit he possessed from his back. He had no serious injuries except shock and a cut nose. This incident installed even more hatred and bitterness for Catholics.

As the mid-1970s approached, Billy found himself saying, 'There is no God'.

5

Turning-point

In 1977 Billy was admitted to the Belfast City Hospital with internal bleeding due to excessive drinking. He was told that his liver was enlarged and that he was a chronic alcoholic. 'You will die within two years if you don't stop drinking,' the doctor told him.

Billy did not accept that he was an alcoholic and believed in his heart that if the troubles in Northern Ireland ended so would his excessive drinking. After a blood transfusion and treatment lasting about ten days he was sent home and warned by the doctor not to have any more alcohol.

Around this time Billy was picked up by the RUC, taken to one of the local police stations and questioned about a very serious crime that had happened in his area. After being questioned for most of the night he was released about 7.30 a.m. the following morning. On another occasion he was taken from his flat by the Army and RUC and questioned about another very serious crime. He was released after many hours of questioning by different detectives.

In 1978 he was readmitted to Belfast City Hospital, vomiting and passing large clots of blood. The doctor who had treated him the previous year was unsympathetic. His attitude seemed to be, 'If you want to commit suicide then go ahead but you're not going to waste my time'. After more blood transfusions and treatment from another doctor Billy was told that his liver was shrinking and hardening up, and that if he continued to drink he would be dead inside a year. The doctor pleaded with him to attend the Shaftesbury Square Hospital which dealt exclusively in drying out alcoholics.

Billy refused to go because he felt the hospital was for drinkers of Brasso, meths and antifreeze. At the time he drank nothing but the best whiskey, vodka and sherry. 'Why should I associate with those down-and-outs in that alcoholics' hospital?' he thought.

He promised the doctor that if he let him go back home he would do his best to stay away from alcohol. Inevitably this did not last for very long. He managed five long weeks. 'They were the most miserable weeks of my entire life.'

On Easter Tuesday morning Billy was standing in the paramilitary headquarters on the Shankill Road with some of his colleagues. It was the day of the Junior Orangemen's March. As they approached with the bands playing he looked across the Shankill Road and saw some of his drinking partners going into the bar. He told his colleagues that he was going over for a drink but they pleaded with him not to go as he would kill himself. Later that day he finished up very drunk.

He began to accept that he was going to die. He could not stop drinking, and the pain in his side was so intense that he started to pass out everywhere he went. He finished up in hospital many times but always discharged himself the following morning.

In June 1979 Billy went on the Whiterock Parade with the Orange Order. That day he could not drink much whiskey because he felt so ill. People noticed him staggering around. In fact his cirrhosis of the liver was causing him to lose his sense of balance and he collapsed four times during the parade.

He had promised his wife that he would take her and his daughter Rhonda to Butlins Holiday Camp in July, but he was so sick with the continual consumption of alcohol he refused to go. His wife did not realize at the time just how ill he was and she and their daughter left for their holiday. Alone at home, Billy drank whiskey all that day. He had a basin beside him on the floor and each time he took a slug from the bottle he was immediately sick. This continued until about 5.00 a.m. the following morning when he collapsed in a heap on the living-room floor, with a terrible burning sensation in the back of his neck. Billy realized he was dying and was terrified.

He remembers crawling to the telephone and with a great effort dialling the emergency code. The ambulance arrived but he does not know how they got into the house as the front door was locked and he could not stand up to open it. The next thing he knew he was in the reception area of the Mater Hospital, Belfast. He heard a doctor tell a nurse to take his blood pressure, and the nurse reply, 'I can't get any reading'. The doctor sounded his heart which was beating very irregularly. Billy started to panic and was given an injection.

For the next ten days Billy was delirious and saw all kinds of hellish, devilish, satanic hallucinations.

One day, lying looking up at the ceiling, it seemed the whole thing collapsed on top of me. The whole ward was a mess with pieces of the ceiling lying around it. I started shouting dirty names at the medical staff. I was confined to a bed with sides on it. I was ripping needles out of my arms when the hospital staff tried to feed me intravenously. One day I turned my head around to look at something behind me and suddenly hundreds of bats flew out of the wall and hit me straight in the face. I felt the pain of their sting.

One evening some men came into the ward carrying booze with them which consisted of beer and shorts. They sat down at the bedside of an old priest who lay in the opposite bed to mine. I watched them open the drink and consume it. Two of them got up and went out of the ward and came back with a coffin. I watched in horror as they lifted the old man out of the bed and put him into the coffin. I thought to myself, 'My God! They're going to steal this old man's body and he isn't even dead'. They then lifted the coffin and started to carry it out of the ward. I began to scream at the top of my voice for someone to stop them. I saw them coming back into the ward with the coffin and putting it on the bed. One of the men lay beside it and began drinking. I remember thinking 'My God! I can never get away from this cursed drink!' The next day my wife came up and I told her about this terrible event. Nothing would quieten me until she got the Sister to remove the screens that were round the priest's bed and let me see he was still there, and not in a coffin.

Two ministers visited Billy while he was in hospital. They read from the Bible and prayed for him, but he was unresponsive. Because of all the violence, bloodshed and suffering that so many people he knew were going through, he did not believe that there was a God. He could not accept that a loving God would let him go through this sheer hell of alcoholism.

Billy alternated between 'sensible' days and 'batty' days. One day his sister May brought him a bunch of red roses. As soon as she came through the doors of the ward he could see blood dripping from the flowers.

I couldn't wait for her to leave the hospital so that I could get rid of them. I called a nurse and asked her to take the flowers over to the old priest's locker. She refused and I became very upset. To calm me down she did remove the roses and put them on the priest's locker as I asked. A few days later he died and I thought to myself, 'It's a good job I got rid of those flowers or that would have been me who died and not the priest'.

Billy was lying staring across the ward one night when something appeared at the foot of his bed. He thought to himself, 'What's it going to be this time?' Somehow this was different. It was spiritual, something supernatural that he could identify with God. Suddenly his whole life flashed in front of him in a matter of a few seconds. He had often heard that before a person dies they see the kind of life they have lived. What he saw was horrible – how he had treated his wife and daughter, his brothers and sisters and other members of his family. He also saw the wasted years of his life in the paramilitary organization, his self-centred attitude over alcohol.

I hadn't cried for as long as I could remember, and I was never sober enough to have any remorse about my actions. However, on this particular night, 24 July 1979, I wept and cried out: 'Lord Jesus, do you think you could ever find it in your heart to forgive me for all the terrible sins I have committed since I left you as a boy of sixteen?' The answer came back that if I was truly sorry and repented I would be forgiven. I cried out for mercy and forgiveness, and at that moment a great burden was lifted from me. I felt a great release and sense of peace.

Billy prayed: 'If you allow me to live I will serve you, Lord Jesus, for the rest of my life.'

He knew that if he should die that night he was now ready to meet God. At that moment God made it clear to him that he was going to be made well, to stand as a witness that Jesus has the power to change people.

He drifted into a peaceful sleep, the first for a long time. The next morning the doctor came to see him accompanied by some student doctors. 'How are you this morning Mr McIlwaine?' Billy told him about the previous night's experience with the Lord. The doctor scratched his head and looked at the students as though he thought his patient was still delirious.

Billy felt that he had to talk to someone about his new experience. A short time later a Catholic nun came down the ward. Billy stopped her and asked, 'Do you believe in God?' She replied that she certainly did, and Billy related what had happened to him. The nun seemed to believe him until he asked her to help get him out of the hospital. He still had the appearance of a very sick and dying man. The doctor later confessed to Billy that he had not expected him to live for more than a few days after his admission. That was why they were prepared to put up with his ranting and raving. Even though the nun had been sceptical about his healing she did see the doctor for him, and was instrumental in getting him out of hospital a few days later.

Billy had no decent clothes in which to leave hospital and he had to borrow some from his nephew. He now wanted to go back home and be with his wife and daughter. He had pawned everything he had to buy alcohol, even borrowing and stealing to satisfy his craving.

I realized that alcohol had been the master of my life: it had told me what to do, when to do it, and how to do it. Thank God I left hospital with a new determination to fight against the power of alcohol.

Billy spent the next few months convalescing at home, reading the Bible and praying.

One verse of scripture that became very important to him was from Paul's letter to the Philippians: 'I can do all things through Christ who strengthens me.' And Jesus did give him strength to get through some very difficult times.

Billy well remembers the first day he left home after his illness. He was walking very slowly down to the office where he worked on the Shankill Road as Chairman of the Black Taxis Association, when he approached a small bar where he used to drink. He began to shake and sweat as he looked across the Shankill Road; it seemed as if the bar was the size of the Empire State Building. It was like a powerful magnet drawing him across the road. He started to repeat the Bible verse: 'I can do all things through Christ who strengthens me.' He managed to get past the bar and along to the office, where he stood trembling and sweating. He could not do any work and went back home a short time later. As the weeks went by Billy became stronger and the bar became smaller.

Every so often he had to go back to the hospital for check-ups. At each visit the doctor was astounded by the healing and the progress in his body. A year after his discharge, the doctor could find absolutely nothing wrong with him, and told Billy that he was totally amazed at how healthy he was.

> I believed God had given me his word that he would heal me. I accepted his word and he fulfilled it. I was now ready to keep my promise to God and tell everyone about what he had done for me.

Billy went to the Paramilitary Headquarters on the Shankill Road and told his colleagues about his conversion to Jesus Christ. He remembers their reaction: 'What! Billy McIlwaine! Never!' He told them that he would not be back within their ranks because he could no longer condone violence in any shape or form.

Some of his former colleagues were sceptical and bet each other that Billy would not last very long as a Christian. More than five years later Billy can still say:

> I love the Lord Jesus more each day. My hatred for Catholics has turned to a real, genuine love for them. I have travelled the length and breadth of Ireland telling them how Jesus changed my life of misery and violence to one of love and joy.

Instead of being a soldier of a Loyalist paramilitary army, Billy is now a Soldier of the Cross, spreading the gospel of Jesus to all men and women of violence.

> I have a special love for all paramilitaries, both Catholic and Protestant, as I realize now how the devil used us to murder each other.

6

For Better for Worse

Late one night in July 1979 there was a knock on Sally McIlwaine's door. It was an old friend of Billy's.

'I was up seeing Billy in hospital tonight,' he said. 'He's seen the Light. He's become a Christian!'

Sally's first reaction was that he must be wrong. Billy was surely delirious; he was imagining things. But the man explained that when he had seen Billy he was not delirious.

'He was as sane as you or I.'

The man was not a Christian, but he knew how important this news would be to Sally.

She went to bed and wondered if it was possible that all the years of heartbreak could be swept away. Was it possible that a hardened drinker such as Billy McIlwaine could be changed so dramatically? She hoped that the news was true.

Sarah McClure, known to everyone as Sally, was born in Belfast on 6 June 1943. The youngest of eleven children she lived in the York Road area. Her father was a military man and the upbringing was strict, yet Sally loved her parents very much.

At the age of nineteen Sally decided to go to work in America. She found a job as nanny with a Jewish family who were very kind to her. In America she met Billy's sister, Margaret McIlwaine, who was homesick for

Northern Ireland. They became good friends and shared an apartment. Sally discovered that Margaret's brother Billy was in Africa with the British Army and would like a pen-pal, so she decided to write to him. Their friendship grew and Sally went out with Billy for the first time when she and Margaret came home on holiday.

> I suppose you would call it love at first sight, but we seemed to get on very well together. At the end of my three weeks, Billy asked me to marry him, and I said yes.

Back in Belfast after their marriage, Sally went out to work with another of Billy's sisters, Ella, who was a committed Christian. Ella started to tell her about being a Christian, and Sally would say,

'But Ella, if I was a Christian I would have to be a hundred per cent, I would have to be perfect.'

Ella had a great influence on her, the influence of a truly Christian life.

Sally knew in her heart that she should commit her life to God. In 1972 when her sister Maggie was dying from cancer, Sally prayed a prayer promising God that she would become a Christian if her sister was healed. But Maggie died and Sally did not become a Christian.

By this time Billy had started to drink heavily. Sally used to go with him for a drink until their daughter Rhonda was born. She just wanted to be a mother and a wife. She had had her fling in America, where she had had a great time. Now she was ready to settle down. But Billy had no such plans. He started to go out by himself and join his friends in the bars. His drinking got steadily worse. After her sister died, Sally felt very downhearted and looked for a way to improve things at home. She decided that moving house was the answer, so they sold their house to the Northern Ireland Housing Executive and temporarily moved in with Billy's mother.

Although Sally loved her mother-in-law and got on well with her, this arrangement did not work well. She was embarrassed to confront Billy in his mother's home. Billy's mother could see that he was drinking more and more and neglecting his family. She used to say to Sally,

'You're too good for him. Why don't you and Rhonda go and live with your sister in America?'

But this was not God's plan for Sally's life and she thanks God that she never left Billy.

Eventually, they moved into a house in North Belfast. Sally thought that things would be better away from the Shankill Road. But the situation got considerably worse, and she was left with the baby while Billy went out and got drunk night after night.

> I realized I made a mistake trying to move away from the kind of life Billy was leading. I thought that taking him away from his friends and associates, the bars and the clubs, he would change. But he just seemed to get in deeper and deeper.

Sally began to get very depressed on her own in the evenings. She had dreamed about being a housewife and mother with a lovely home of her own. Now it seemed that her world was falling apart around her, as she realized that her dreams were not going to come true.

Ella kept urging her that she needed the Lord. The Lord would sort out her problems if she trusted him. Sally had few close friends to confide in, and she did not want to let her family know what was happening. At times she felt close to breakdown.

One night in January 1974 Sally was on her own at home with Rhonda when one of Billy's sisters telephoned to say that their mother had died. Billy loved his mother very much and Sally was extremely concerned that now he would do just what he liked. His mother would have been very cross with him for treating her the way he did. When eventually Sally told Billy about his mother's death he was heartbroken.

By this time buying another house was out of the question, so Sally had been searching for a house to rent. At the suggestion of Billy's family, Sally went to see the man who owned his mother's house. With tears in her eyes she explained that they had been looking at houses which were all too expensive. Could they rent the house Billy's mother had lived in? The man told her that he was selling all the property he had, and did not intend to do any more renting. Sally's heart sank as she wondered where she was ever going to get a deposit for a house. Nobody would ever give them the money for it. The man looked at her and said:

'If you give me £50 as a deposit for the house, and £14 a month rent, will that do?'

Sally was overjoyed.

After Billy's mother died, Sally had no peace. She could not sleep properly; she could not eat. At last she took the Bible out of the drawer and started to read it. Sally had such conviction about giving her life to God that she could ignore it no longer. She thought she was going crazy, but she puts that experience down now to being convicted by the Holy Spirit. At 7 o'clock in the morning of 15 February 1974, Sally came downstairs and said out loud:

> Lord, I can't take any more. Please help me. You know what Billy's like and you know everything about me. Lord I need you.

She did not feel very different inside: no great joy, still worried about the mess her life was in. Still she went immediately and told Ella, who lived just round the corner, that she had become a Christian. Ella was delighted.

'Sally, I had everyone praying for you.'

Sally appreciated the fact that people cared enough to pray for her. She was also surprised by Billy's reaction when she told him the news:

'I thought that was going to happen because you've been reading the Bible!'

Sally found a source of help and strength in her new Christian faith.

'I thank God for the Holy Spirit, the Comforter, because I just couldn't have gone through what I did if it hadn't been for him.'

Billy's drinking got worse, and whenever he came home his language was terrible. Sally had to restrain herself and not say anything, because if she did it always ended up in a big argument. At night Billy would fall asleep easily, but she couldn't.

'I would go to bed in tears and lie in bed on my own. It wasn't a marriage at all.'

Gradually, Sally became involved in her church. She helped in the Sunday school, and became an officer in the Girl's Brigade. This took up a lot of her spare time and took her mind off her domestic problems.

The police and security forces came more than once and searched the house. Sally prayed to the Lord that Rhonda would not wake up. She was only a little girl, and her mother just could not bear to think that she might open her eyes and see members of the security forces in her bedroom. The tears ran down Sally's face whenever they entered the house.

I'd be lying in bed alone, and then suddenly there'd be a knock on the door. I was afraid. I didn't know who it would be. Fear built up inside me. It might be somebody with a gun.

During these times Sally was strengthened by her faith in God.

Sometimes things got so bad that Sally found that she was unable to pray. It was at times like these that Psalm 61 became very special to her:

Lead me to the rock that is higher than I.
For thou hast been a shelter for me,
and a strong tower from the enemy.

Whenever Sally read these verses she felt they had been written especially for her. She could not pray. She was so overwhelmed that all she could do was cry.

Very early one morning the security forces came to the house, and a special branch detective sat her down.

'Where's your husband?'

'I don't know.' (This was true. She always told Billy not to tell her anything. If she knew nothing, she would not have to tell lies, and so break her promise to the Lord. Her conviction was so deep that she would have seen Billy go to prison before telling a lie.)

The man seemed to understand. Sally cried.

'I'm a Christian. My husband and I live two completely different lives.'

He looked at her: 'You know, I believe you.'

Sally did not know what they were searching for in the house. When Billy came back, he went to the police station and asked if they were looking for him. They told him to come back again on Monday. Still very shaken, Sally realized that this had been a security check in the area.

Her prayers were answered because Rhonda never woke up when there were people in the house, and never once saw the security forces. But the little girl was starting to grow up and beginning to notice what her father was doing. Sally worried when Billy came home and took no interest in his daughter. She had to try to be a mother and father to her. It was very difficult. Sally found that her experiences as a nanny were useful as a parent.

> I wanted Rhonda to be able to speak to me, to be open. It wasn't like that with my parents, who were very old-fashioned. I wanted Rhonda to be able to come to me with her problems, tell me anything that was on her mind. I was concerned that she shouldn't turn against her father. I wanted her to love him.

This was difficult because Sally found that she was fighting a battle within. Her heart was turning against Billy. Her love for him had slowly drained away. She could not see any future for them in the way things were going. It got to the point where she began to hate him, although as a Christian she knew that she should not hate anyone. It was happening slowly and she did not realize it.

On Sunday morning a friend gave Sally and Rhonda a lift to church. On the way he challenged Sally:

'You're going to have to love Billy more than you ever loved him, even when you married him, because it's only love that's going to conquer all this.'

Sally prayed and asked the Lord to help her to love him again. It was not easy. There was one embarrassing incident when Billy followed her into church drunk and dishevelled. He sat at the back of the church and Sally could hear the whispers, 'Billy McIlwaine's in, Billy

McIlwaine's in.' She wanted the ground to open up and swallow her.

> I knew what he would be like; he had drink on him, and I felt the shame of it. I couldn't help feeling like that. Then the Lord seemed to speak to me, and I asked him to help me go and sit beside Billy.

The service had begun, but Sally got up and sat beside him. He made an excuse that there had been a telephone call from America and that he had just come to the church to let her know. She firmly believed that the Lord was working in his life and had brought him to church. When they got outside Billy went straight to a drinking club.

During all this time Sally was under great stress and strain trying to hold down a job and keep the house together. Sometimes Billy would go out and not come home for a couple of days, or even a week. She knew Billy was an alcoholic but she could not speak about it freely at the time. She did not know who to go to. There was a growing belief in Sally's heart that Billy would indeed come to share her Christian faith, but she had a strong premonition that it would be on his deathbed.

There were times when Sally visualized herself a widow, and thought that she and Rhonda would be happy then. She prayed daily that Billy would have a meaningful experience of Jesus Christ before he died. One day she realized that she was praying with the wrong motives. It dawned on her that she was not wanting Billy's life changed for his own benefit, but because it would make things easier for her. She started to pray that the Lord would save Billy in his own time and way.

When Rhonda was eight she came in from school one day. Sally was lighting the fire.

'Mummy, I've something to tell you.'

'What is it Rhonda?'

'Mummy, I'm a Christian!'

Sally was very touched, and started to cry. Her face became black with soot as she wiped the tears away with her dirty hands.

'What made you decide?'

'Mummy, you're going to heaven and I want to go with you.'

Sally was thrilled, but she realized that Rhonda hardly ever mentioned her father. Yet as Sally's love and compassion for Billy grew, so did Rhonda's. When Billy was asleep, the sweat used to run down his face and his bottle of whiskey would be by his side. The compassion in Sally's heart would rise. She would take a handkerchief to wipe the sweat off his face, and kiss him when he was asleep. Rhonda started to copy her mother. She wiped her father's face when he was asleep and she kissed him goodnight even though he knew nothing about it. She prayed for him every day.

By 1977 Sally felt in need of a complete break. Her older sister in America invited her to bring Rhonda to stay with her in Philadelphia. She saved every penny for a year and managed to get enough money together for the flight. In 1978 she and Rhonda spent six weeks in America during the summer holidays. The result was surprising. Billy realized how much he missed them, and they realized how much they missed him even in the state he was in. Billy telephoned Sally every other night all the time she was away. Sally came home to an enormous telephone bill, but she realized that Billy needed her and his daughter.

'I knew then that I still loved him and still wanted him.'

Sally wrote to Billy nearly every day she was in America and she prayed that he would be kept safe. He sometimes fell asleep with a lighted cigarette in his hand. Sally had left a Bible in the living-room, and Billy later told her that there were many times when he wanted to pick it up and read it, but was afraid. He knew he would discover in it the truth about his wasted life.

Billy was never without a drink. He didn't go to pubs any more because people could not put up with his nasty behavior. He hid bottles everywhere in the house, and Sally was driven to the point of telling him that if he wanted a drink he should be open about it and have one.

He was ruining the furniture by hiding bottles all over the place. They leaked and the house was beginning to smell like a distillery. One night he needed a drink and didn't have one to hand. He'd such a bad pain in his side that he couldn't walk very well, so he asked me if I would let Rhonda take him to the off-licence. I refused. My heart was just breaking at the thought that he depended on drink. I knew it was a disease and only the Lord could cure him. So out of compassion I took his arm and went with him. Maybe some people would think that wasn't right, but rather me than Rhonda.

Sally stood outside the off-licence and waited for Billy to come out. As they were walking home, Billy turned to her and thanked her for going with him. Now Billy didn't normally thank Sally for anything: he did his own thing and if that didn't suit her, well tough luck. Could this be the first hint of a change of attitude?

Billy had promised to take Sally and Rhonda on holiday to Butlins not long after this, but when the time came he said he was too sick to go. Sally was tired of going to hospitals with him, tired of calling doctors round, and whenever he said there was something wrong she no longer believed him. This time she sat down beside him and very calmly said,

'Billy, when I come back from Butlins I'm leaving you. You can stay in the house and I'll not take anything, but I'm taking Rhonda and going away, and I won't be back.'

Billy just looked at Sally. To this day he does not even remember her saying it to him.

Sally and Rhonda went to Butlins in the South of Ireland. Sally was not happy and next morning she telephoned the house to see if Billy was all right, even though she had decided not to go back to him. He was not there and so she telephoned a girl who worked in his office.

'Sally, I've got bad news for you. Billy's in hospital.' Sally's first thoughts were, 'This is the end. Billy's going to die.'

She didn't know whether to be glad or heartbroken. A friend brought her back to Belfast and when she arrived at the hospital Billy was seriously ill, raving and in the DTs.

Sally prayed, 'Lord, don't let him die without you.'

Then came the night when Sally heard that Billy had become a Christian. Next morning she went to see him in hospital and asked if he had anything to tell her. Billy looked at her for a moment.

'What d'you mean?' he said casually. 'That I've become a Christian?'

When Billy came out of hospital and went back to work, there were still doubts in Sally's mind. If he was more than a few minutes late home she would imagine him in the pub. But slowly things improved.

> I was really very happy. But it still took time for our marriage to come together. We had to get used to each other again. It was a special time when Billy and I knelt down by our bed, held hands and praised God together for what he had done for us. In the past Billy would swear at me and mock me when I prayed. It's great to be able to share your life again. It's even better than it was when we first got married. Today we're serving God together as a family.

7
Soldiers of the Cross

Billy's life was no longer in danger through his weakness for alcohol. But his decision to share his new Christian faith with former paramilitary colleagues created another threat.

It is not possible just to leave a paramilitary organization. The only way a person can leave is by a genuine conversion to Jesus Christ. Some people might try to use Christianity in a wrong way but they are making a big mistake. You must be genuinely converted and live that type of life. There is no way that I know of that you can go to the paramilitaries and say that you are fed up and have had enough. Once you swear the oath of allegiance to that organization you're bound by it. If you say you don't want to be involved with the military operations they might put you on to the welfare side of the organization.

If they see that a man has genuinely converted to Christ they usually leave him alone. They've a set code of what a Christian should and shouldn't do, especially on the Protestant side. You shouldn't smoke or drink. You shouldn't curse or go with other women. You shouldn't go to dances but you should go to church. If you are not seen to be living that kind of life and continue to go to pubs and clubs, they would say that you are not a genuine Christian. They would insist that you go back to the meetings. One man did try to pull the wool over their eyes and he finished up dead.

Billy said that he would be willing to die for the name of Jesus.

I'm not saying that I wouldn't be afraid; we all have human fear. But I will not run away from my responsibilites as a Christian. I will stand up for the gospel, no matter what the stakes may be.

Billy knows that his life is always in danger now that he is a Christian. In 1980 he was under a death threat. Two men arrived at his office in the Shankill Road on a motorbike. He knew the trade mark of assassination. He saw the motorbike stop outside his office and the pillion passenger look around him and put his hand down to feel the gun. He realized at once that this was going to be an assassination attempt. He ran into the back office, locked himself in and telephoned the police. In a very short time he heard a banging on the door and someone said, 'Open up, this is the police'. He thought it was the gunmen pretending to be the police. He said a short prayer. 'Lord, my life is in your hands.' He opened the door and the RUC were standing there. Billy was very shaken.

An article, *God's Army Beats The Terrorists*, published in the Sunday Press, reports a conversation between Billy and reporter Paddy Reynolds.

'I supported the Loyalist cause actively. I'm not saying I killed anybody, but for ten years I was a full-time paid member of a paramilitary organization.'

The reporter then asked how Billy squared his past with his conscience, now that he was born-again? As a committed Christian did he not feel the necessity to make a clean breast of everything and take the punishment that was due to him like a man?

Billy's reply raises important issues: 'It is a question that I am often asked. I fervently believe that God has forgiven me for everything I have done and for which I have sincerely repented. Prison is meant to reform. It is also meant to remove from society those who are a menace to it. Society is in no danger from me. I believe God has given me a mission in life to preach the Gospel of Jesus Christ to all men.'

He was asked how he justified his connection with the 'black taxis' which at one time were synonymous in the eyes of a lot of people, including the security forces, with many of the activities of the outlawed UVF (Ulster Volunteer Force). Billy replied: 'It is true, of course, in the old days black taxis were engaged in bombing, shooting and murder missions. But since I took over as chairman of the Shankill and Shore Roads Black Taxis Association, things have changed. They are all properly insured and comply in every respect with the law. I am paid by the taxi men themselves.'

On 16 August 1972, the UVF in Belfast arranged for a local taxi service to run from Protestant estates. They charged the same rates as the corporation buses. A statement from the UVF said that the bus service 'left much to be desired'. At the start twenty taxis took shoppers into the city centre. By 1984 there were ninety black taxis on the Shankill and Shore roads.

Billy told me that he did not think anything would be achieved by his going and confessing to the RUC anything that he might have done in the past while a member of a paramilitary organization. 'God has forgiven me for everything that I ever did, he said. 'I also believe that I can be far more use outside prison trying to create a peaceful solution to the problem of Northern Ireland.'

In 1982 Billy and others organized a gospel mission in the Ulster Hall, Belfast. Just before the campaign started in October he received another death threat.

One night he was stopped and told that an attempt was going to be made on his life. Someone from a particular organization had sent a message that he was to be eliminated. He shared this with two pastors and asked them to pray for him. One of them had a vision of a dark shadow hanging over his life. He was advised to call the gospel campaign off but he refused. He said that he was not turning back because he had a duty to God to go on with God's work in Northern Ireland.

Billy continued with the preparations for the meetings, and the assassination attempt never materialized. The pastor sent word to him that the 'cloud' that had been hanging over his life had lifted.

The gospel campaign was a great success and among the many men and women who found new faith in Jesus Christ were a number who had been members of terrorist organizations. Knowing at first hand the pressures and problems of born-again ex-paramilitaries, Billy saw the urgent need for some kind of fellowship to support and encourage them. A group of them met together in a house in East Belfast on 29 October 1982. They decided that the fellowship would be known as the 'Soldiers of the Cross'.

The Ideals and Aims of the Soldiers of the Cross were decided on. These are:

1 To promote the gospel of Jesus Christ to all paramilitaries.
2 To encourage all ex-paramilitaries who have become Christians.
3 To visit and encourage all Christian prisoners.
4 To share the gospel with all prisoners.
5 To promote good relationships between ourselves and the families of serving prisoners.
6 To work and pray for peace in our country through the power of Jesus Christ.

7 We believe that through his death Jesus Christ cleanses us from all sin and binds us together in Christian unity.

8 To establish further fellowships.

At the time of the founding of the Soldiers of the Cross one Northern Ireland newspaper report said:

> The Shankill butchers are high on the target list of a new group formed last week. But the Soldiers of the Cross will be armed only with a Bible when they confront the cut-throats who still send shudders down the spines of Belfast Catholics.

One of the people who has helped and encouraged Billy since he became a Christian is the Rev. Jim Hagan, minister of Woodvale Presbyterian church in Belfast. After the gospel meetings in the Ulster Hall, Billy shared with Mr Hagan his burden to start a fellowship for ex-paramilitaries who had become Christians. The minister was most impressed when he heard Billy speak, and became interested in the Soldiers of the Cross, 'Because there is a genuine setting aside of old tribal hatreds and an acceptance and love of people from the other side of the divide'.

Mr Hagan is now chaplain to the Soldiers of the Cross fellowship, which holds its regular Tuesday evening meeting in his manse on the Woodvale Road. He feels that Billy is making a contribution to peace and reconciliation in Northern Ireland by showing people what it means to be a Christian.

> Only people who live in the Shankill or Woodvale Roads know the risks that he's taking in declaring that he loves all men equally. It's hard to come out of a paramilitary background like Billy has done and continue to live in an

area where the paramilitary organizations are strong. His former paramilitary colleagues know the stand he takes. They know Billy of old, and they know that only God could have done what has taken place in his life.

The founding of a Christian group for ex-paramilitaries soon became news. In January 1983 people in Britain came to hear about the Soldiers of the Cross through an article, *Breakthrough in Bomb City*, published in *Buzz*, a Christian magazine for young people.

Sectarian savagery and a seemingly endless legacy of blood and tears have forced many Christians to avert their gaze from the city of Belfast. Yet God is moving amid the bullets, fear and hatred. Paramilitaries have come to Christ. The spirit of healing and reconciliation has begun to move.

Buzz editor Steve Goddard flew to 'Bomb City' himself and wrote:

All may not be gloom and despair. Stories of Bible studies in the Maze, Crumlin Road and Magilligan prisons and former Loyalist paramilitaries holding revivalist-style missions in the notorious Shankill Road and Belfast city centre have filtered through. Several Ulster Defence Association men convicted of lesser crimes who found Christ 'behind the wire' are now free and have willingly given their testimony to packed congregations at Elim Pentecostal churches.

As a result of this article, *20/20 Vision* made a thirty-minute television documentary, *Soldiers For Christ*. Reporter Jackie Spreckley introduced the programme:

In Northern Ireland there is a new and extraordinary movement for peace amongst the very men and women from both sides of the religious divide who were once at the heart of the sectarian violence and hatred. They are paramilitary soldiers who put down their guns and turned to Christ. They found forgiveness for their former enemies. Catholic for Protestant. Loyalist for Republican. They are born-again Christians.

Billy was interviewed:

I belonged to an organization that did carry out murders. Even if I didn't pull the trigger myself, the very fact that I belonged to that organization makes me as guilty as the men who did pull the triggers. I don't think that there is anybody in Northern Ireland who can truly say that they are innocent of any blood.

The Soldiers of the Cross is a peaceful movement. The paramilitary armies are violent movements. We are trying to create a situation where men will come to accept Jesus Christ, to accept the Prince of Peace and to create peace. To get men to go across the divide to shake hands with their Catholic neighbours rather than go across to shoot them. We have been in various parts of Belfast where I would never have gone while I was a member of a paramilitary organization.

Jackie Spreckley told viewers:

I have just been inside Magilligan Prison and witnessed something which I wouldn't have believed was happening unless I'd seen it with my own eyes. There were men in there serving sentences for terrorist crimes coming together in prayer and praise of the Lord. Both Catholics and Protestants are putting behind them their former hatred for their enemies, and finding love and peace in their hearts through Jesus Christ.

At the end of the programme Billy said that there were people who would like to see him back in the organization. Back in the ways of violence. He was grateful to God that he could be happy trying to promote the gospel of peace.

Mary Smyth, an ex-member of the Provisional Republican Movement, joined Billy to speak at a Celebration for Pentecost in St Patrick's Cathedral, Dublin on 22 May 1983. Earlier, more than 8,000 people from all parts of Ireland, including over 1,000 who came from Northern Ireland, took part in a two-mile march through the city streets from St Stephen's Green to the Cathedral. The Rev. Cecil Kerr, director and founder of the Christian Renewal Centre at Rostrevor, Co Down, gave an address in which he put into words the belief that inspires the Soldiers of the Cross: 'Even if we had a perfect political solution tomorrow we would still be left with the problem. For the heart of the problem is the problem of the human heart.'

The leaflet about the event reminded people of the spiritual side of Ireland's agony. It quoted a promise in the Bible's Second Book of Chronicles: 'If my people who are called by my name humble themselves, and pray and seek my face, and turn from their wicked ways, then I will hear from heaven, and will forgive their sin and heal their land.

While they were in Dublin, Billy and Mary appeared together on the *Late, Late Show*, Irish television's most prestigious and popular chat show. They answered questions about how they had left paramilitary organizations and become Christians.

In August 1983 the first newsletter of the Soldiers of the Cross gave encouraging news of a fellowship underway and practical help being given. A minibus given by a Christian businessman was in use by families in several different towns to make visits to the Maze high-security prison, near Belfast.

During October 1983 Billy was approached by two women whose husbands were implicated by an informer. They knew that his views as a Christian put him against the use of informers.

> I knew from one of the first 'supergrass' trials that a particular person was telling lies. This made me think about the morality of using informers. I felt that the whole judicial system in Northern Ireland would come into disrepute. People would be lifted, interrogated and put into prison and there would be no justice left.

Billy chaired a meeting in a hall in the Shankill Road, attended by about thirty women. The name 'Families For Legal Rights' was adopted at his suggestion. Billy was asked to become chairman and a committee of six people was formed. At a further meeting, a decision was taken to meet with a Catholic group formed at about the same time, called 'Relatives For Justice', to see what the two groups could do in common. A joint meeting was held in the Europa Hotel, now re-named the Forum, the most bombed building in the centre of Belfast.

It was a very positive three-hour meeting with people representing each group. They decided to hold a joint Press Conference in the hotel on 9 November. But after the Darkley atrocity things broke down. It helped to sway the feelings of some people who did not really want to sit down with Republicans. They felt that by meeting with Republicans they were defeating the cause of Loyalist men in Long Kesh who were fighting for segregation from Republican prisoners.

Billy insisted that he loved all men and women and would fight for the rights of everybody. The 'supergrass' system had affected Catholics as much as it had affected Protestants.

So as not to hinder his work among Catholics, Billy resigned his membership of the Orange Order and the Royal Black Institution. The Orange Order, founded at the end of the eighteenth century, is the largest Protestant organization in Northern Ireland. Today it has approximately 100,000 members. Based on secret lodges like those of the Masonic Order, it holds marches and parades throughout the Province each twelfth of July. This is to celebrate the defeat of the Catholic King James II by his successor William of Orange at the Battle of the Boyne in 1690.

Billy has already been invited to speak in America, Britain and Europe. The 'Peace People' travelled a lot in their time, but Billy does not feel that he should leave Ireland at the moment. If he were to leave Ireland and visit other parts of the world, he could easily lose the vision and the burden God has given him. The work is in Ireland.

At a half-night of prayer at his own Zion Tabernacle in Canmore Street, Billy felt that God was calling him to prayer and fasting in order to seek his will.

The Soldiers of the Cross held their first conference at the Ballyholme Hotel in Bangor on 5 November 1983. Billy chaired the meeting which was attended by more than seventy people. Church of Ireland, Methodist, Presbyterian and Pentecostal ministers and a Catholic priest were among those present to hear Protestant and Catholic former paramilitaries describe the change in their lives.

Billy explained how the Soldiers of the Cross got its name. It was taken from one of the apostle Paul's letters: 'Endure hardship with us like a good soldier of Jesus Christ. No-one serving as a soldier gets involved in civilian affairs – he wants to please his commanding officer.'

He also described how the fellowship began. It was not until a dinner arranged by an international Christian Businessmen's group that he met former Republican paramilitaries and a real bond of friendship was established between them.

Billy then told the conference that he had been criticized by some people for using the media. He did not want publicity for individuals but he did want it for Jesus Christ. To show how effective the media could be he told how one day a woman came up to him and said, 'Billy, I heard you speaking on the news the other night about your gospel campaign in Belfast. A friend of mine came round as a result of hearing you and asked me to show her the way to Jesus Christ.'

A few weeks later, just four days after the Mountain Lodge shooting, I went with Billy to Armagh where we had a meeting lasting more than two-and-a-half hours with Cardinal O Fiaich. I had told the Cardinal earlier about Billy and the work of the Soldiers of the Cross. Billy told him how God had changed his life from one of violence and hatred to one of love and peace. It was a very positive meeting. At the end of it the Cardinal prayed. He prayed for Billy and his work with the Soldiers of the Cross. He prayed for the victims of the Darkley killings. He prayed for Ireland that peace and reconciliation would come through the power of Jesus Christ. He then invited Billy to pray. Billy was very impressed by the sincerity of the Cardinal. He found him a very open man.

Early in 1984 the Cardinal spoke about the powerful witness of the Darkley widows.

No one who heard an interview with one of the bereaved Darkley families or with their pastor could fail to be inspired by their profoundly Christian attitude in the midst of grief, by their deep and living faith, by their absolute confidence in God's mercy and love and by their Christ-like forgiveness for those who wronged them so grievously . . .

Three courageous Darkley widows and their family circle seemed to soar above the petty dissensions and bickering which had marked the path of Christian disunity for far too long, and pointed the way towards ultimate unity in mutual acceptance of each other as children of God.

While the ex-paramilitaries were at prayer during their conference, they came to believe that the Lord was speaking, telling them that Ireland was going to be released from the cloud of evil which at present hangs over it. Jesus was going to use the very men and women who had committed the violence to be ambassadors bringing peace and reconciliation.

One such is a man whose friendship and advice Billy values very much: Jackie Gourley. A staunch Protestant from a staunchly Protestant area of Belfast, he joined a Loyalist paramilitary organization when the troubles started, because he wanted to run all the Catholics out of Ulster.

'Although I was an atheist, God had his hand on me even then because I never killed or bombed anyone.'

The last time Jackie was arrested he was charged with carrying a gun and received a three-year prison sentence. He was released in 1976, a year before a good friend who had received a five-year sentence on a hijacking charge. In 1978 Jackie heard that this particular friend had become a Christian. He was very sceptical and treated it with contempt, because he thought his friend had only become a Christian to get out of the paramilitary organization.

Jackie met his friend who told him that he had become a Christian and invited him to go to church with him. Jackie says:

As an atheist I hated God. I hated Christians. I hated everything to do with religion. I hated everyone, including myself. I remember sitting in a bar one day looking at my pint and saying: 'Is this my life? Is this going to be my future just sitting here drinking day after day? Going home, fighting with my wife Shirley and getting thrown out of the house?' I should have told my friend that I wasn't interested in going, but I said yes.

Jackie went with his friend to a Pentecostal church in Belfast. He had heard the gospel as a boy at Sunday school, but this time it was different. During the service he felt very nervous and wanted to get out of the church as fast as he possibly could. His friend asked him to go again the following week.

I went with my wife, but I was a bundle of nerves when I left the church and smoked incessantly on the way home. The Holy Spirit must have put me under great conviction because in bed that night I was so troubled that I prayed for the first time in years. I said: 'Lord Jesus Christ please be my Lord and Saviour.' He didn't cast me out. He just put his arms around me and loved me.

That was on 2 April 1978, and two weeks later his wife Shirley also became a Christian.

Now Jackie wanted action. It was not good enough for him to put his Bible under his arm and shout 'Hallelujah'. Together with four other Christian friends, he formed a singing group called 'The King's Sons'. Jackie still hated and shunned all Catholics.

I treated all paramilitaries like scum and didn't want anything to do with them. When Billy asked me to join the Soldiers of the Cross, Jesus gave me enough love to open my heart and my arms to all paramilitaries and ex-paramilitaries.

8

'Blessed are the Peacemakers'

It is not widely known that there have been a number of large conferences in Ireland, North and South, attended both by Catholics and Protestants. One such was in September 1976, in Dublin, with more than 5,000 Catholics and Protestants present from all over Ireland. Among the speakers was David Watson, one of the Church of England's best-known evangelists; his theme, 'Blessed are the Peacemakers'.

One of our first responsibilities as sons of God is to become peacemakers. 'Blessed are the peacemakers, for they shall be called sons of God.' As sons of God we are to make peace. But it may be a very risky business. It will never be easy. It will demand endless patience, persistent love, and constant forgiveness. It will lead to threats and intimidation. It may cost some even their lives. Therefore, to be effective in any lasting way we shall certainly need to work in the power of the Holy Spirit.

In the tremendous struggle in which God has placed us, we really do need one another. We need each other's support and prayer and love. We cannot go it alone. We cannot go it alone within our own tradition. That is why, through the cross of Jesus Christ, God has pulled down all the barriers between us. Whatever tradition you and I may come from, when we come to the cross of Jesus Christ and open our hearts to the life and power of the Holy Spirit, there is nothing between us.

Just over seven years later, in the same week as the Darkley killings, David Watson made the last of his many visits to Northern Ireland. He was extremely ill with cancer. He spoke at a Festival of Praise in the Presbyterian Assembly Hall in Belfast.

We need to listen to one another and learn from one another. Fifteen to twenty years ago my attitude towards Catholics was almost as hard as anyone's. While I was in hospital earlier this year, some of the letters which helped me most, which pointed me most to Jesus, were from Catholic friends.

The following day David Watson spoke in a Catholic church in Dublin. This was to be his last Festival of Praise on Irish soil. He died of cancer at his London home in February 1984. He was just fifty.

David did not spare himself during his visits to Ireland. In the North he visited prisons and talked to hardened terrorists, Protestant and Catholic, about the healing love of Jesus. Some responded, and renounced violence and hatred, and committed their lives to Jesus.

Billy attended the service of Thanksgiving and Celebration for David Watson's life held in Belfast that April. Protestant and Catholic churchmen took part. The Rev. Cecil Kerr called the congregation to declare in faith and in hope, that declaration of victory which David taught us in Psalm 89 – *The Lord Reigns*.

9
Mary Smyth

Mary Smyth, an ex-member of a Republican paramilitary organization, became a committed Christian in April 1979.

Mary was born on 8 December 1943, at Tullyvallen Cullyhanna, Co Armagh in Northern Ireland. She was baptized in the Catholic church and given the names Margaret Mary. Her father was a small farmer and he and her mother worked very hard to provide for their family. As she grew up Mary enjoyed helping her father with the animals. During the summer holidays from school she spent the days in the fields helping to harvest the crops.

Mary's father would sometimes tell her of his activities with the 1st Northern Division IRA between 1917 and 1921 and in Sinn Fein, (the political wing of the IRA). As a result of some particular operations in which he had been engaged against the British Forces, he had been on the run from his home for some time. After the signing of the Anglo-Irish Treaty in 1921 he became disillusioned with politics as he saw some of his comrades become party politicians in the twenty-six counties of Eire and abandon the six counties of Northern Ireland to the mercy of the Unionist government at Stormont.

Always a man of religious tolerance, he had good relationships and lifelong friendships with his Protestant neighbours and associates in the farming community.

However, growing up in the North of Ireland the family was always conscious of being Catholic. They were strict in their observance of Sunday Mass and the sacraments of the church and always had family prayers morning and night in their house. All Mary's education was received in Catholic schools.

Perhaps to some extent her father's involvement in the struggle for independence contributed to her early interest in the politics of her country. She liked to listen to his occasional reminiscences of some of the exploits of those years of active resistance against the British forces. Mary's early years were also influenced by a young priest who was very keen to promote the Gaelic language and culture. She joined his dancing and language classes. In July 1955 she was to attend a Gaelic language course but a few days before she had a serious car accident which sent her instead to Daisy Hill Hospital in Newry.

I was given the Last Rights of the Catholic church. I suffered some loss of memory for a time due to concussion. I listened to the bands of the Orange Order assemble and parade for the twelfth of July celebrations. Listening from my hospital bed to 'Dolly's Brae' and 'The Sash', I was aware of my feelings of resentment towards this antagonistic celebration. It was little wonder that Catholics felt isolated from the rest of the population and alienated from the society in which they lived.

For Catholics the result of the 'marching season' was a deepening resentment and an inevitable anger, coupled for many with a resolve to do something about it.

Mary was aware that an IRA offensive was taking place against the British forces throughout the period

1950–62. Although she was very young, she already identified with their efforts. She listened intently to news broadcasts of sabotage attacks against various installations and raids on barracks, such as Armagh and Brookeborough, the latter claiming the lives of IRA Volunteers Sean South and Fergal O'Hanlon. In 1955, a young Catholic named Arthur Leonard was returning home from Confession in the church when he was shot dead and his girlfriend seriously injured by the B Specials near Keady, Co Armagh, only ten miles away from Mary's home. (The B Specials were an armed part-time force who helped the police with security duties.) This caused further resentment towards the security forces locally, and particularly towards the B Specials. The incident made a deep impact on Mary and she later realized she was already becoming bitterly anti-Unionist and anti-British, although still only twelve years old.

> People over a wide area of the countryside mourned the loss of Arthur Leonard, seen as a victim of the prejudice of our society in Northern Ireland. Perhaps there were Protestant people saddened too, although we would have doubted their sentiment, such was the nature of our cynicism. Certainly we experienced a good caring relationship among neighbours, but there never seemed to us to be a dissenting Protestant voice in the area of politics.

Ever since Mary was a young girl of nine or ten years old, she enjoyed music and singing of all kinds. She took a special interest in Irish ballad singing and traditional music. Many of the songs she learned from them were about times of distress and rebellion in Ireland – so much of Ireland's history is tragic and so much of it is written in song. She knew the songs of the 1798 Rebellion and the 1916 Rising. The music which accompanied those rebel songs was either militant or plaintive and would always waken deep emotion in her heart.

Feelings of hatred towards the British who had ruled Ireland by force or arms, crushing rebellion after rebellion. Those songs fuelled my own feelings of rebellion and gave me hope that the spirit of Irish Republicanism would one day soon cause the people to rise again. Britain was retreating from one colony after another. Would her oldest colony soon be relinquished too?

Occasionally Mary managed to get hold of the Republican Movement's newspaper, *The United Irishman*, which was banned in Northern Ireland. Through reading it she became aware of the role of women in the Republican struggle at all levels. She knew that there would come a time when she too would take her stand in the cause of liberty and national freedom.

Catholics on leaving school had little or no hope of finding employment. Dole queues were growing and the only alternative was emigration. Mary had attended Our Lady's Grammar School in Newry. She took a Civil Service examination early in 1961 and hoped to get a post in Northern Ireland. This did not materialize, and her posting was to the Air Ministry in London. She was not altogether surprised and suspected her overseas appointment was due to her being a Catholic. She resented this and decided to turn down the appointment and emigrate instead to the United States.

In May 1961, at the age of seventeen, Mary flew from Dublin Airport to Boston to join her uncle, his wife and family in Portland, Maine. Her first job, which she found immediately, was in a Portland insurance company office. Very soon Mary had made some friends who helped her to adjust to the new American lifestyle. Maine is known as Vacationland in the United States and has a beautiful summer climate which she particularly enjoyed. She did not find it easy to be totally cut off from her own generation of Irish people. The only native Irish in Maine had been there, like her uncle, for thirty years and were out of touch with Ireland. Many of them had not even been back home since they emigrated.

Mary knew some friends who had emigrated from Ireland to New York and later in 1961 she decided to join them there. Mary began work in the office of her new employer, the world's largest stock brokerage firm of Merrill, Lynch, Pierce, Fenner & Smith Inc in the Wall Street district of Lower Manhattan. She found living in New York City challenging if not sometimes at least intimidating. The teeming masses of people pouring into and out of the subway trains and offices were a stark contrast to the peaceful tranquillity of a South Armagh hillside. She knew that the widespread unemployment in Ireland meant that she must be content with the opportunity she had to work in the States. But she missed her family and the Irish lifestyle.

Many Irish people of her generation were coming to New York and as a result they were able to form a very close-knit community. There were many sporting and social events which she enjoyed, and in addition she had a special interest in the South O'Hanlon Club which was formed in association with the Republican Movement in Ireland.

We engaged mainly in demonstrations aimed at highlighting the injustices of British rule in Ireland and of getting American support for resistance. Living for some time on the fringe of Harlem, New York's infamous black ghetto, I witnessed the prejudice and poverty which so often and in so many ways reminded me of Northern Ireland and gave me a close identity with the Black Civil Rights Movement of the 1960s.

Mary received newspapers from home which kept her in close touch with the political situation in Northern Ireland. The ending of the IRA campaign around 1962 brought about an amnesty for political prisoners in the Crumlin Road Prison. Some of these men were later to emigrate and Mary became acquainted with them through the South O'Hanlon Club. She was painfully aware that the social and economic conditions, coupled with the prejudice and injustice which the Catholic people were feeling, would eventually spill out into frustration and anger. She could see the hardline attitude of Unionist politicians had polarized feelings and alienated the Catholic community.

On 12 February 1966, Mary married Brian Smyth, a native of Scotstown, Co Monaghan. Her husband was not interested in politics, though he accepted her deeply held beliefs and did not interfere. Like Mary he was prepared to return to live and work in Ireland. In April 1967 they came back to Ireland on the last transAtlantic voyage of the Queen Mary.

Brian took a job with a building contractor in Portadown, Co Armagh, and they began to search for a house to buy. They looked at every house which came onto the market around Lurgan but found the area extremely polarized. They could hardly believe how divided the people were after their years away in the United States. Brian and Mary could not buy the houses which became available week after week because they were apparently in Protestant areas of the town and the sellers advised them against buying since they said the neighbours would attack the house and force them out.

This was 1967 before the start of the present troubles in Northern Ireland, but it indicated the fragility of the society and the degree of latent hostility. Eventually they succeeded in buying a house in a new mixed area of mainly business and professional families. After spending the summer of 1967 there, Mary was in no doubt whatsoever that they were sitting on a powder keg. 'All the ingredients were present for a violent outburst,' she says. 'It only needed something insignificant to spark it off.'

Captain Terence O'Neill had earlier taken over from Lord Brookeborough as Prime Minister of Northern Ireland and had taken a new course. He had travelled to Dublin and opened dialogue with the Dublin government for the first time since the establishment of the Free State. They planned to work together on matters of mutual concern: agriculture, industry and tourism.

Prime Minister O'Neill had recognized the dangerous consequences of the previous policy of Unionist government, and he was attempting to defuse the explosive political situation. I felt that his efforts were too little and far too late.

The Catholic people were becoming more determined on political reform and an end to the gerrymander of constituencies, unfair housing allocation and the appalling religious prejudice in employment. A combination of these factors led to the formation of the Irish Civil Rights Association on 24 August 1968, with a march from Coalisland to Dungannon in Co Tyrone. Mary welcomed this movement and supported the marches, which were also organized in Armagh, Derry and Newry. Now, through the stand being taken by the Civil Rights Movement, the passive mood of Catholics was being replaced by a demand for action and a growing militancy brought about by the failure of the Stormont government to implement the long-awaited changes.

In 1968 Mary and her husband moved to Co Monaghan in the South to live on the farm where her husband had grown up. The farm is close to the border with Co Fermanagh. Shortly after the move her mother-in-law died. In April 1970, Mary and her husband had their first son, Kieran, followed two years later by another, Declan.

Mary joined the Provisional Republican Movement early in 1970 and in her own words became 'steadily more involved and committed to it over the next eight years.' She believed in the *Eire Nua* (New Ireland) programme for political, economic and social advancement put forward by Sinn Fein. She was certain that only the complete overthrow of British rule in Ireland could pave the way for a democratic Socialist Republic in Ireland. She also believed passionately in the need for national liberation if the Irish people were to have any chance of a Gaelic language and culture revival. She believed the injustices in the six counties could only be dealt with in the context of a New Ireland which guaranteed political and religious freedom to all its citizens.

'I was prepared to risk life and liberty in order to see my vision fulfilled,' she says. Her family suffered ill-treatment and harassment by members of the security forces in the six counties and in the twenty-six counties, and one of her brothers was imprisoned in the Irish Republic. The reactionary violence of the state only succeeded in solidifying her opposition to the authority of a state which seemed to her to use repressive means to maintain its authority.

As I saw it, the six counties were being held by Britain illegitimately at the point of the gun, and the only way to bring about their annexation was therefore to match force with force. The IRA campaign of bombing and inflicting economic penalty on Britain was a necessary part of the war of liberation.

The most difficult aspect of the deaths during the troubles for me and for Republicans in general was the sectarian conflict. I despised the idea of Irish people, Protestant or Catholic, killing each other and the deep division caused within the community as a consequence. I believed that the British government was taking advantage of the sectarian conflict as their justification for being in Northern Ireland and for using the Army to carry out police duties. I believed that if the military presence was removed, Protestants and Catholics would have to face the new reality and negotiate terms agreeable to each other.

In the early 1970s one form of British government succeeded another in Ulster. But to Mary whether they were Labour or Tory made no difference. No progress was being made towards a permanent settlement of the age-old British-Irish question. The two communities in Northern Ireland, Catholic and Protestant, were growing further apart each year while the British Government seemed content to settle for what became known as 'an acceptable level of violence'.

Mary expresses her position at that time: 'I was fully committed to a long drawn-out offensive by the Provisional IRA.'

10
Changing Allegiance

In April 1979, Mary's life took a radical new direction. During a casual visit to her doctor, Mary asked for a precautionary cancer test. Her doctor discovered a large tumour in the left breast. The following Tuesday morning, Mary had an appointment with a surgeon at Our Lady of Lourdes Hospital in Drogheda. Her doctor's obvious concern made her feel very alarmed and despondent.

She remembered how less than a week earlier a businessman who called at her employer's office in Monaghan mentioned the Charismatic Renewal Movement in the Catholic church to her. Mary had asked him many searching questions about this movement, which looks to take the church back to a full dependence on the Holy Spirit, as at the beginning. But she had dismissed any suggestion of going to meetings, which he told her took place each Monday night in Monaghan. Now that invitation took on new meaning, and she realized that she could go to the meeting on the night before she was to be admitted to hospital.

> Throughout that week, every hour of each day seemed to get darker for me as I thought of the possibility of the large tumour in my breast proving malignant. I was faced with the stark reality of death. In bed at night I couldn't sleep and I would tremble all over with fear. I couldn't bear the thought of leaving my children and it terrified me to think of them growing up without a mother.

Mary was sceptical of the Renewal Movement in the Catholic church, but she decided to go to the meetings hoping to get the strength to face the hospital and the surgery which terrified her. She was greeted by a young priest, Father Ronnie Mitchell, a native of the Falls Road area of Belfast. The meeting began with hymn-singing, accompanied on the accordian and guitar.

It seemed strange at first as the thirty or so people present enthusiastically sang joyful songs, not the type she was familiar with in church. Between songs, some-one would open a Bible, read a few verses and share what the Holy Spirit was saying; some gave thanks for help received through prayer. Father Mitchell then gave a short teaching on the theme of 'expectant faith'. Mary had never heard the term 'expectant faith' before and she listened attentively as he invited them to pray 'expecting' God to answer their prayers and supply their needs. He then laid hands on each person who re-quested prayer and prayed with them, Mary included. The meeting concluded with short Bible readings and more joyful singing.

Mary left the meeting clinging to the 'expectancy' and thanking God in anticipation of what he was doing in answering her prayer for healing. The joyful songs continued to ring through her mind and she felt they had replaced the fear that had previously gripped her. Next morning, without giving any reason, Mary asked the children to remember so say 'Thank you, Jesus' throughout the day.

Mary felt very peaceful and even joyful as she and her husband travelled the seventy miles to the hospital. She sang the songs and related the experience of the previ-ous night and together they gave thanks to God. On arrival at the hospital, Mary was given a bed and had to wait a considerable length of time before the surgeons came. During all this time she was relaxed, confident and because of the joy in her heart she was in fact smiling, something which she thought fascinated the hospital staff. Finally the surgeon arrived and carried out a full examination. He could find no evidence of the tumour still being present!

The surgeon gave Mary several examinations and check-ups during the next six months but the result was the same.

> God had intervened. The healing power of Jesus Christ had come into my body just as surely as when he healed the many sick people when he walked as a man on this earth nearly 2,000 years ago. I realized the truth of the verse from the Bible: 'Jesus Christ is the same yesterday and today and for ever.'

The next Monday evening Mary returned to the prayer meeting to give thanks for the miracle of healing. After the meeting she bought a copy of the Bible. That she believes to have been the most important and significant step she has ever taken in the course of her life, although it was not immediately evident. Under the advice of Father Mitchell, Mary sought the guidance of the Holy Spirit in prayer each day before she read the Bible. Before long what had seemed to her like a dry history book became so alive and powerful that she did not want to put it down.

> There were many great moments as the Holy Spirit revealed more and more of the truth, but perhaps the most significant day was when I was struck by the apostle Paul's words, 'While we were yet sinners Christ died for us'. This was truly the day of my conversion. I found the reality of God's love for me. The condemnation and judgement which

I had felt from the church had caused me to become embittered, but I knew then that it hadn't come from God but from man. Jesus taught that we should hate the sin but love the sinner, just as he did. This reality became the transforming force which was to bring me to the foot of the cross, convicted, broken, sorrowful, repentant and changed drastically.

Through studying the Bible and praying, I was lifted into new heights of love and joy and peace. I found that the old desires which had controlled and dominated my life were becoming a memory, a memory which I was horrified even to recall. I couldn't believe that my heart could ever have harboured such evil thoughts and murderous conspiracy. I was overwhelmed by the extent of God's love and forgiveness. I now desired only to love the very people against whom I had conspired. Instead of the hatred which I had towards the British security forces and the RUC, I now had deep compassion and forgiveness.

God had given me a new heart and new eyes. Through repentance I became reconciled with him and with my enemies. I pondered how a short time before my desire had been to see my country free. Now I had found new freedom deep inside myself. By comparison the cause which had seemed so urgent now seemed so empty, so unimportant. I had found the 'pearl of great price'.

I had experienced the greatness of God's love through his all-embracing forgiveness. I now knew if I was to follow him, if I was to be a Christian, then no matter how great an offence anyone committed against me, I must likewise forgive. I had to change. I had to be prepared to admit publicly that I was wrong, and one of the hardest areas to admit to was my political beliefs which I had held for some twenty-five years. I surrendered my life to God prepared to allow him to continue to change me.

Mary was well aware of the significance and stigma attached to a Republican abandoning the struggle which she had been bound under oath to uphold. She had to risk being labelled and suspected as a traitor. But she could no longer in conscience support any organization engaged in killing. This she saw as contrary to the law of God. When Jesus said 'Love your enemies and pray for those who persecute you', he did not qualify it or make it optional. And so she made her decision for Jesus Christ and resigned from the Republican Movement.

Mary does not judge or condemn her former comrades, but longs that they also will find the freedom which she found in Jesus Christ. Through Renewal she has experienced a liberating sense of being filled with and led by the Holy Spirit. She believes God is saying to her: 'I have allowed you to know my healing power in your body and to experience the transforming power of my love in your heart. Now go and be a witness to my mighty power that I may heal your land.'

Choosing to become a committed follower of Jesus Christ, Mary found herself in a new war-zone. This time the battlefront was within her – between her ways and the ways of God made known to her by the Holy Spirit. She discovered that living according to the gospel of Jesus was the most radical, revolutionary life she could lead. It was a constant state of warfare, battling against the flesh, the world, and the devil, all of which combine to build the kingdom of darkness.

In the past she had looked on the injustices which the Catholic people in Northern Ireland suffered.

I experienced the utter contempt Protestants had for us and my reaction was resentment, anger and rebellion against them and the British authorities who allowed it. I was committed to replacing this unjust system with a socialist government in Ireland which would give Catholic, Protestant and dissenter equal rights and liberties. I believed that it was justifiable to use whatever means were necessary in order to achieve this ideal. Today, I know this was Satan's deceptive trap and I was caught in disobedience and rebellion against God's laws. I have come to see Nationalism, Unionism, Republicanism, Loyalism and Socialism as potentially idolatrous, replacing in our lives and hearts the priority of God and his laws.

Jesus Christ told us there are two spitual systems, the kingdom of god and the kingdom of Satan, Each of us works to build up one or other by the way we live daily. I soon recognized that the real enemy at work in our society was Satan, the source of all evil. Bigotry, injustice, anger, rebellion and war all belong to him, all originate with him. I knew Satan had used me to serve him. I had allowed him. He entered through the resentment and anger in my heart.

By repentance, Mary had turned away from Satan and turned back to God seeking forgiveness. She accepted the gift of reconciliation with God which Jesus had made possible by his life, death and resurrection. The Darkley massacre stood as an example of her totally new way of seeing things:

The killings at the Moutain Lodge church at Darkley may appear as a defeat to some. For me, Mountain Lodge is a spiritual victory over the demonic forces which inspired men to attack it. All around Ireland Christians wept and sorrowed together at the loss of their brothers in Christ. People weren't waiting to read the denominational tag of the victims. It was unimportant. As the Bible tells us, 'If one member suffers, all suffer together'. Neither were they waiting to condemn the attackers, but instead they united in prayer that God's mercy would lead them to repentance.

Mary takes part in weekly prayer meetings with people from other Christian traditions. They are held in Monaghan, a town just a few miles south of the border with Northern Ireland.

> We meet as Christians together to pray and share the Bible. These meetings have been very important in helping us to grow in understanding and appreciation of our different traditions. For some it was their first opportunity to share and pray with people from the Catholic tradition. It was also a new experience for many Catholics to share with Protestants whose knowledge of the Bible is especially beneficial to Catholics who are encouraged to begin Bible reading. All of us meet respecting each other's customs, not imposing our own preferences but seeking to be of one accord, united by one Spirit in the body of Christ. There are many barriers to surmount and much we need to learn about each other.

Before his death in the Darkley massacre, they were joined in prayer by David Wilson, one of the elders who was killed at the Mountain Lodge church, and by other members of the congregation. David Wilson was, Mary believes, the heroic example of a person stepping out in faith to build 'bridges of love' across denominational and territorial barriers. She sees that many people have been inspired through the forgiving love of that congregation and the bereaved families. The challenge she feels is for all of us who follow Jesus Christ to leave behind the darkness and division of the past, so that the victory of Christ over Satan may be publicly seen in Ireland.

> We need to ask ourselves individually, 'am I willing to allow God's healing power to act in my heart, to change my attitudes?' Young people are disillusioned with a society rampant with injustice, unemployment and exploitation, resulting in the satanic curses of alcoholism, drug addiction

and hopelessness. We need to become zealous for Jesus Christ as St Patrick was when he came to us, a foreign and a pagan people. He came in love, with the good news of God's love, and people responded. Their lives were transformed by faith in the healing power of Jesus Christ. By the working of the Holy Spirit the seeds planted produced abundant fruit. We became renowned as 'the island of saints and scholars'.

The enemy of Ireland is not the British Army, the RUC, the Orange Order, the IRA, INLA, or the UVF. The enemy is Satan seeking to use every channel he can. There is hope for the people of Ireland. That hope is in Jesus Christ who loves and cares for each person uniquely, who died for each one of us. We who know Jesus Christ, and who know his power to transform lives, must be prepared to stand in the fray as Soldiers of the Cross.

The living Lord Jesus cares about Ireland and about the problems wo face. He asks all of us today to recognize that the cancerous sickness of our society is the direct result of our sin, our selfishness. He calls all of us to acknowledge our spiritual sickness, that we need to come to him. The churches, I believe, have allowed the political crisis to distract them from leading and guiding their people locally to respond to people's needs across political and denominational barriers.

In contributing to this book there has been much agonizing which I endure for the sake of Christ and the people of Ireland. I believe, however, it is God's will that I share my thoughts, and for his sake I pray that among you who read, some may ponder and find new purpose in life.

11

'I Forgive You'

The violence of the paramilitaries has ensured that Northern Ireland stays in the news. Usually the victims remain silent. But the widow of Inspector Harry Cobb of the RUC hit the headlines. Mrs Florence Cobb wrote to Leo Green, the Provisional IRA terrorist serving a twenty-five year sentence for her husband's murder, forgiving him. In a television interview in May 1983, Mrs Cobb said that it had taken her a long time to write the letter. The Lord had given her a great concern for the young man. There were times when she sat down at the table to write the letter, and just could not get the words for it.

But in the end she wrote it, and this is part of it. It is dated 24 November 1980:

I write not to condemn you or be critical of you in any way. I believe that my husband's appointed time had come, his work here was finished and God called him home to be with himself. He was ready to meet God. I long that you might make preparations to meet God too. You see, everyone of us has to stand before God and give an account of what we have done with God's Son. In a personal way we each decide either to accept God's offer of mercy and take Christ as our Saviour or to reject him. I pray daily that God might open your eyes and the eyes of your fellow inmates, Republican and Loyalist, Catholic and Protestant, religious and irreligious to see God's Son bleeding and dying to save you.

Florence Cobb told me she is still praying that the Lord will speak to Leo Green and that one day she will get a letter back to say that he too has accepted Jesus Christ into his life. By mid 1984 Mrs Cobb had still not received a reply but she has not given up hope. Inspector Harold Cobb was murdered at security barriers in Lurgan, Co Armagh, on 24 February 1977.

In the same television interview Florence Cobb, a mother of three who lives in Hillsborough, Co Down, revealed something even more amazing. She is to marry Kenny McClinton, a convicted double-killer described by a judge as a 'cold-blooded and completely ruthless assassin'. Kenny is a former Loyalist paramilitary, who has become a Christian while serving a life sentence in the Maze high-security prison near Belfast. He and Mrs Cobb have become engaged and plan to marry when Kenny completes his sentence.

Kenny wrote to Florence Cobb when he heard her speak on the BBC *Sunday Sequence* programme in September 1981. He said in his letter that he had become a Christian. Three months later, after several letters, she began to visit him. Her three children have also been to see him and they all love him. They support their mother in her relationship with Kenny and look forward to the day when he is allowed to come home and become a part of the family. Florence Cobb explains the kind of thing that made her warm to this man with whom she had come in contact in such an unusual way:

Jesus died for people like Kenny in the Maze, for those in Magilligan and those in the Crumlin Road and Armagh prisons. Kenny isn't using his Christianity to try and get out of prison early. He sees the Maze as his mission field and we are both prepared to wait to get married until God's perfect time. Kenny is being used of God in a mighty way in the Maze and he has had the joy of pointing prison officers and prisoners alike to Jesus Christ.

In March 1983 Kenny almost lost his life when he was attacked by fifteen Republican prisoners in a tea-hut during a tea-break. A bucket of boiling water was thrown over his back and he was severely beaten about the head and body with hammers rolled up in cloth and with lengths of wood.

It was only by the grace of God that Kenny was able to escape from his assailants as no prison staff were present when the attack took place. While lying in the prison hospital in great pain from the severe burns which he received he asked to see the priest, who was chaplain to the men who had attempted to murder him. Through this priest Kenny conveyed his forgiveness to those who had planned the evil against him and assured them of his prayers for their conversion to Jesus Christ.

In the prison hospital Kenny had to have skin grafts on his back.

Kenny McClinton was convicted of two murders in 1979 and received two life sentences with a recommendation from the judge that he serve at least twenty years.

In a letter to Billy from H-Block 7 in the Maze Prison, dated October 1982, he wrote: 'Your story has been a constant source of strength and encouragement to me, and many others within Ulster's prisons.'

Kenny was arrested in August 1977, charged with a number of serious terrorist offences and remanded to Crumlin Road Prison. He was made commander of a paramilitary group inside the prison, and as such applied himself to the disruption of all penal activities in an attempt to win political recognition. He was moved to the H-Blocks in the Maze where he immediately resumed the battle.

Within the next nine-month period he was sent to the punishment cells on fourteen different occasions. For between fourteen and twenty-eight days he was in total isolation from the other prisoners. While a man is 'on solitary' he is placed in a bare white-walled cell devoid of any means by which he might pass his time away – no radio, newspapers or books. Nothing, that is, except a Bible.

I began reading the Bible, initially because I had nothing else to do and through a certain curiosity as to just what this old book contained. Soon I was thoroughly enjoying the Old Testament stories of war and intrigue. Then I came to the New Testament and witnessed the love which Jesus Christ – the Son of the living God – had for his sinful people. Things were never quite the same after that.

Kenny returned to Belfast for trial and on the first day of February 1979 a High Court judge said something like this to him: 'McClinton, I find that you are a cold-blooded, callous and completely ruthless man. You are in fact an assassin. I sentence you to life imprisonment on two counts and recommend that you serve not less than twenty years.'

Kenny was brought back to the H-Block among all his old penal adversaries, only this time it was as a Loyalist blanket protester. His Bible reading continued in his new solitary world, but this time it was a diligent search for the truth.

While on remand, I'd lost the woman I'd lived in sin with as my wife. I'd lost the two children whom I loved. I'd lost the house which I'd built up over the years. Now the judge had taken away twenty years of my freedom. I was left with nothing, nothing but the clothes on my back and an indomitable human nature, black with sin and guilt. The protest took the very clothes off my back and left me bare in the eyes of God. I'd no hope and I was spiritually bankrupt.

A spiritual battle began in my heart. It seemed as though the Holy Spirit was engaged in a battle with Satan for the prize of my unworthy soul. By 12 August 1979 I could ignore God's calling no longer. My 'no surrender' became 'total surrender', to the love of God. Jesus Christ forgave me my sins as I knelt there on the prison floor.

12

Hopes for a New Ireland

The political background to Northern Ireland has come into this story from time to time as the stories have unfolded. What is happening on the political front now? In 1983 the Irish government initiated the 'New Ireland Forum'; their report was published on 2 May 1984. All political initiatives in Northern Ireland up until this time had failed. In the short term the prospects for the ideas contained in the Forum report provide a glimmer of hope. Long-term they provide the best political opportunity the Province has had for peace and stability since its inception in 1920.

Billy and Mary are both convinced that the only long-term peaceful solution in Ireland is a change of heart by all men and women, an utter rejection of violence and an acceptance of real life-changing Christianity.

The Forum lacked the necessary unity of both Catholic and Protestant politicians when it opened in Dublin Castle on 30 May 1983. In the event, only the three major political parties in the Irish Republic – Fine Gael, Fianna Fail and the Labour Party – took part, together with the mainly Catholic Social Democratic and Labour Party from Northern Ireland. The Unionist parties refused to take part in the proceedings. They want Northern Ireland to remain an integral part of the United Kingdom, and were totally against talks which might undermine this. Individuals representing a Unionist point of view did send written submissions and those invited appeared before the Forum to answer questions.

The Forum received a total of 317 submissions from both parts of Ireland, from Britain, the USA, Belgium, France and Canada. They reflected many views, including those of the nationalist and unionist traditions, and covered a wide spectrum of topics – economic, social, political, constitutional, legal, religious, educational and cultural.

One section of the report, *The Cost of Violence from the Northern Ireland Crisis since 1969*, highlights the urgency of the crisis:

> The most tragic loss is that of the deaths of over 2,300 men, women and children. These deaths in an area with a population of 1½ million are equivalent in proportionate terms to the killing of approximately 84,000 in Britain or 350,000 in the United States of America. In addition, over 24,000 have been injured or maimed. Thousands are suffering from psychological stress because of the fear and tension generated by murder, bombing, intimidation and the impact of the security measures. During the past 13 years, there have been over 43,000 recorded separate incidents of shootings, bombings and arson. There is hardly a family that has not been touched to some degree by death, injury or intimidation.

Not surprisingly the report states:

> The immediate outlook for the North is extremely dangerous unless an acceptable political solution is achieved. The long-term damage to society worsens each day that passes without political progress. In political, moral and human terms there is no acceptable level of violence.

On 9 February 1984 a delegation representing the Catholic Bishops of Ireland appeared before the

Forum. Bishop Cahal B. Daly of Down and Connor made their opening statement:

> The Catholic Church in Ireland totally rejects the concept of the confessional state. We have not sought and do not seek 'a Catholic State for a Catholic people'. We believe that the alliance of Church and State is harmful for the Church and harmful for the State. The Catholic Church in Ireland has no power and seeks no power other than the power of the Gospel which it teaches and the consciences and convictions of those who freely accept that teaching. The Catholic Church seeks only the freedom to proclaim the Gospel of Our Lord, Jesus Christ . . .
>
> We are acutely conscious of the fears of the Northern Protestant community. We recognise their apprehensions that any political or constitutional or even demographic change in Northern Ireland would imperil their Protestant heritage. It is not for us to formulate proposals for constitutional change or to draft blueprints for a future Ireland. That is the business of legislators. What we do here and now declare with emphasis is that we Bishops would raise our voices to resist any constitutional proposals which might infringe or endanger the civil and religious rights and liberties cherished by Northern Protestants.

In a key chapter, *Framework for a New Ireland*, the Forum comes out clearly with its favoured pattern for the future. It speaks emphatically of civil and religious liberties and rights being guaranteed, no discrimination on grounds of religious belief, government and administration sensitive to minorities, consensus. But then, against this background, the report states clearly:

> The particular structure of political unity which the Forum would wish to see established is a unitary state achieved by agreement and consent, embracing the whole island of Ireland and providing irrevocable guarantees for the

protection and preservation of both the unionist and
nationalist identities.

The report notes in some detail two other pos-
sibilities: a federation or confederation of the two parts
of Ireland, with local parliamentary structures for each
under a national government, and a form of con-
dominium under which a Northern Ireland executive
would be invested with authority jointly by London and
Dublin.

Irish Prime Minister Dr Garret Fitzgerald showed his
open approach to the Forum report during President
Reagan's visit to Ireland in June 1984. He described it as
'an agenda, not a blueprint'.

What are Billy McIlwaine's considered thoughts on the
New Ireland Forum? They reflect mainstream Protestant opinion in Northern Ireland as it was at the time the
report was published. He could not see its radical proposals being accepted by the people of the Protestant
Shankill Road.

The ordinary working man and woman regards the Forum
as interference in his or her affairs. Without consulting the
various paramilitary organizations and at least listening to
what they have to say, the politicians are wasting their time.
When I was involved with a paramilitary organization there
was no way that I would have accepted any report on a New
Ireland. It is only now that I am a Christian that I can even
think about a New Ireland. It does not scare me, but I am
only one among many.

The politicians had no mandate from the people of
Northern Ireland to produce the report. The SDLP are not
representative of the majority of the people. If either
Westminster or Dublin does try to implement any of the

things in the report without the consent of the people it could lead to increased violence and bloodshed in Northern Ireland.

Before anything constructive can be done in our country, people must turn back to God, both Protestants and Catholics. This is something I keep praying and working towards. I try to change people's hardline views by turning them to Jesus Christ.

13
The Way Forward

Many people have put forward formulae for peace and prosperity in Northern Ireland. Each new Secretary of State for Northern Ireland has implemented what he thought would be the way forward. Each of them has failed – not because politics is irrelevant – there are injustices in Northern Ireland, but because changing structures do not change people's deeply entrenched attitudes.

Each successive commander of the security forces has claimed that the paramilitaries were beaten, but no military solution has yet been found. As each paramilitary is jailed so another takes his place.

The Peace People were given world-wide publicity. The founders won the 1976 Nobel Peace Prize. But today there is only a small remnant left of what started out as a great movement of the people of the Province.

So is there any more likelihood of a breakthrough in what is happening with the Soldiers of the Cross? Yes, I believe there is. Because now at last the power is being discovered to change the people of violence themselves.

Converted ex-paramilitaries like Billy McIlwaine and Mary Smyth have renounced violence as the way forward. They say,

There is no military or political answer. The only answer to the troubles in Northern Ireland is to love Jesus Christ. It is only through loving Jesus Christ that we can love our fellow men and women whether they be Protestant or Catholic, and that we can learn to respect each other's traditions.

The politicians in Northern Ireland find very few things that they can agree on. It is now conceivable that Sinn Fein, the political wing of the Provisional IRA, will capture more than fifty per cent of the nationalist vote in future elections. If this happens then moderate Nationalism in Northern Ireland could be finished and the armalite will have triumphed through the ballot box.

What is needed in Northern Ireland today is a spirit of forgiveness. Unless this happens I can see very little hope for our society. There is only hope if people try to forgive each other for what has happened; then a love and bond can grow from person to person. If people don't learn to respect each other and each other's traditions, then our sons and daughters, our grandsons and granddaughters have no future. All they have to look forward to is violence, bloodshed and death.

What has happened has happened because of the evil in the land. Satan has used those amongst us to kill and to maim, deceiving people that they were doing it for a cause. I know how the men and women of the various paramilitary organizations think because I came up that road myself. While I was engaged in that kind of life I never had peace, or joy. I was fighting for something but I didn't know what it was. What did I know about being a Protestant? I didn't know the gospel, and I didn't know God. How many Protestants in Northern Ireland really know Jesus Christ? And what do members of the Republican Movement know about Catholicism? They had no regard for the head of their Church when he came to Ireland in 1979 and pleaded with them to give up violence.

Billy believes that fighting and bloodshed can become such a way of life that sometimes it possesses a person and takes full control of his personality. In the years that he was involved with the paramilitaries he knew men who started out with a cause and finished up as psychopaths, lusting for blood. He is willing to sit down and talk with any paramilitary group in Northern Ireland. In return he asks them to listen to his message.

I appeal to the men and women in the various paramilitary organizations to examine in their hearts what they hope to achieve by violence and bloodshed in Northern Ireland. If your dreams were realized tomorrow, what happens then? I appeal to you: Reconsider your ways of violence. Is there not a better way? Is there not another way than the bomb and the bullet?

I love this country and I love the people of this country. I pray that through what has happened to me and Sally something positive might be achieved, that Catholics and Protestants, Loyalists and Republicans might want to live together in peace. A man does not have to be a Catholic or a Protestant. In the Bible Jesus says: 'Him who comes to me I will not cast out.'

Over the years the churchmen of Northern Ireland, the ministers, the priests, the pastors, the preachers, have not done enough to bring about peace and reconciliation.

How many priests and how many ministers can say in their heart: 'Lord, I did everything I could to ask my congregation to love their fellow men and women?' I challenge the ministers of the gospel from both sides of the community to ask themselves if they have done all they can to encourage their people to be reconciled with their fellow men. For far too long churchmen of various denominations in Northern Ireland have tried to say the things that please their people instead of being men of courage.

The Soldiers of the Cross continue to work with the hard men and women of the paramilitaries both inside and outside the prisons. Billy's aim and Mary's is to preach peace and reconciliation, and to bring the good news of Jesus Christ to all people, both Protestant and Catholic, throughout the whole of Ireland.

And there is a yet deeper level of spiritual resource needed. Those who have been most closely involved in the violence know this best. There is something satanic going on, which makes the apostle Paul's words so relevant:

Put on the whole armour of God, that you may be able to stand against the wiles of the devil. For we are not contending against flesh and blood, but against the principalities, against the powers, against the world rulers of this present darkness, against the spiritual hosts of wickedness in the heavenly places.

On Sunday, 22 January 1984, Pastor Bain told his congregation at the Mountain Lodge Pentecostal church:

'I feel God is in the service this morning. The devil has no part in the service. God is here.'

This was the first morning service since the killings. The congregation gave shouts of acclaim as Pastor Bain commended the hymn 'Are you washed in the blood of the Lamb?' This was what the congregation were singing when the gunmen opened fire on that cold November night two months before.

In the plywood door to the porch a thin layer of white paint covered, without hiding, a circle of seven bulletholes. All the blood-stained hymn-books had been scrapped and there was a new carpet on the floor. Outside, RUC men with rifles slung across their chest, backed up by members of the British Army, guarded the little hall until the last worshipper had left. Life in Northern Ireland goes on. But only the power that transformed ex-paramilitaries Billy McIlwaine, Mary Smyth, Jackie Gourley and Kenny McClinton will bring an end to terrorism.

Appendix 1

Loss of Life in Northern Ireland 1969–84

Loss of life arising from violence in Northern Ireland, 1 January 1969 to 30 June 1984.*

Date	Civilian	Security Forces	Paramilitaries	Unclassified	Total
1969	13	1	1		15
1970	17	2	5	1	25
1971	96	59	17	1	173
1972	242	149	75	8	474
1973	130	79	40	3	252
1974	149	51	21		221
1975	177	31	35	1	244
1976	221	54	19	2	296
1977	55	46	12	1	114
1978	31	31	7	1	70
1979	31	68	5	2	106
1980	42	31	5		78
1981	42	44	19	3	108
1982	39	41	13	2	95
1983	29	35	9	5	78
1984*	9	22	5	2	38
	1,323	744	288	32	2,387

This table was first published by the New Ireland Forum and up-dated by the Irish Information Partnership.

The Cost of Violence arising from the Northern Ireland Crisis since 1969 states in its introduction: 'There have been periods of violence in the Northern part of the island for many years, both before and after partition in 1920. The people of the North, and to a lesser extent of the South and of Britain, have during these periods suffered death, maiming and bombing. The violence has destroyed jobs and economic opportunities.'

Appendix 2
Diary of a Troubled Land

Selected dates in the history of Northern Ireland 1968–84

1968
23 March
Northern Ireland Prime Minister, Captain Terence O'Neill, calls for an end to 'The balance of hatred which is hereditary to us all'.

20 May
Loyalist protesters carry 'O'Neill Must Go' placards outside Unionist function in Belfast.

24 August
First Civil Rights march from Coalisland to Dungannon, to protest over housing allocation. Gerry Fitt, Republican Labour MP, protests about police batonning of Civil Rights marchers.

5 October
Civil Rights Association march in Derry. At Craigavon Bridge protesters batonned by police. Rioting in Bogside.

30 October
Irish Prime Minister, Jack Lynch, meets British Prime Minister, Harold Wilson in London and blames partition of Ireland for recent unrest.

22 November
Captain O'Neill announces a five-point reform programme including a housing points system.

9 December
Captain O'Neill broadcasts his 'Ulster stands at the crossroads' speech and appeals for support for his reforms.

1969
19 April

Serious rioting in Derry. Paisleyites stone Civil Rights supporters.

28 April

Captain O'Neill resigns as Prime Minister.

1 May

Major James Chichester-Clark becomes Prime Minister.

2–4 August

Sectarian violence erupts in Belfast. More than 100 arrests; several pubs and houses set alight.

12 August

Rioting at Apprentice Boys' march in Derry. Petrol bombs used when police break Bogside barricade. CS gas used to disperse crowds: 'Battle of the Bogside'.

13 August

Bogside under siege. Trouble spreads to West Belfast and other towns in Northern Ireland.

14 August

First British troops enter Derry.

15 August

British troops move into action in West Belfast to provide a buffer between Protestant and Catholic crowds on what later became known as the 'Peace Line'.

10 September

Hunt Report recommends replacement of B-Specials with 4,000-strong part-time police force. Guns and petrol bombs seized in Loyalist Shankill Road in Belfast.

1970
10–11 January

Sinn Fein Ard Fheis splits: some delegates declare allegiance to Official IRA, others walk out in support of a Provisional IRA Army Council.

18 June

Conservatives win British General Election

3 July

Five people killed in Belfast in conflict between Provisional IRA and British Army as army imposes curfew on Lower Falls area in Belfast.

23 July

All marches in Northern Ireland banned for six months. Two CS gas canisters thrown in House of Commons in London.

12 August
Apprentice Boys march in Derry despite ban.

21 August
Social Democratic and Labour Party (SDLP) formed in Northern Ireland.

1971
23–24 January
Rioting in Shankill Road in Belfast.

6 February
First British soldier shot dead in Northern Ireland since start of present troubles.

20 March
Prime Minister, Major Chichester-Clark, resigns; succeeded by Brian Faulkner.

14 July
SDLP announces boycott of Northern Ireland Parliament at Stormont.

9 August
Start of internment without trial in Northern Ireland. 300 people arrested by British troops in dawn raids. Twelve people killed, 150 houses burned down during rioting in Belfast.

6 September
15,000 Protestant workers attend rally organised by Rev. Ian Paisley to form Civil Defence Corps.

19 September
Internees moved to Long Kesh.

5 November
Announcement that 882 people have been arrested on internment orders.

4 December
Fifteen people killed in UVF bomb attack on McGurk's bar in Belfast.

1972
29 January
British troops fire rubber bullets and CS gas to disperse Civil Rights marchers in Dungannon.

30 January
Bloody Sunday: 20,000 people attend Civil Rights rally in Derry. Troops from 1st Batt. Parachute Regiment open fire, killing thirteen civilians.

1 February

Prime Minister, Edward Heath, announces Widgery enquiry into Bloody Sunday.

2 February

30,000 people march on British Embassy in Dublin and burn it down.

22 February

Official IRA bomb at Aldershot wrecks Parachute Regiment Mess, killing seven people including five canteen workers.

4 March

Bomb explodes in Abercorn Restaurant in Belfast killing two people and injuring 130.

20 March

Bomb in Lower Donegal Street in Belfast kills six people. Responsibility claimed by Provisional IRA.

24 March

Direct Rule of Northern Ireland from Westminster. Stormont Parliament suspended. William Whitelaw appointed Secretary of State for Northern Ireland.

19 April

Widgery Report exonerates British Army for deaths during Bloody Sunday.

29 May

Official IRA suspends operations in Northern Ireland.

7 July

William Whitelaw has secret meeting with Provisional IRA leaders in London.

21 July

Bloody Friday: Provisional IRA cause twenty-two explosions in Belfast killing eleven people and injuring 130.

31 July

Operation Motorman – British Army enters the 'no go' areas in West Belfast and Bogside in Derry.

1973

8 January

220 special-category prisoners transferred from Crumlin Road Prison to Long Kesh, now officially re-named The Maze.

7 February

Belfast Loyalists go on rampage at end of one-day strike called by Loyalist Association of Workers.

8 March

Two car bombs in London kill one person and injure 180. Responsibility claimed by Provisional IRA.

20 March

British Government White Paper recommends establishment of an eighty-member Assembly elected by proportional representation, executive power to be shared with Catholic minority.

28 March

Irish Navy ships intercept illegal arms haul on Cypriot vessel, Claudia, off Waterford.

28 June

Elections for Northern Ireland Assembly.

31 July

First meeting of Assembly ends in disorder.

2 December

Francis Pym replaces William Whitelaw as Secretary of State for Northern Ireland.

6–9 December

Tripartite London-Belfast-Dublin talks at Sunningdale lead to establishment of Power-Sharing Executive in Northern Ireland.

1974

4 January

Ulster Unionist Council rejects Council of Ireland proposed at Sunningdale.

7 January

Brian Faulkner resigns as leader of Unionist Party.

28 February

Labour wins British General Election called as a result of miners' strike and three-day working week in Britain.

5 March

Merlyn Rees appointed Secretary of State for Northern Ireland.

14 May

Ulster Workers' Council calls general strike. Province brought to a standstill. Collapse of Power-Sharing Executive.

17 May

Thirty people killed in four Loyalist bomb explosions in Dublin and Monaghan.

29 May

Ulster Workers' Council call off strike.

10 October

Labour wins second British General Election.

21 November

Provisional IRA bombs in two Birmingham pubs kill twenty-one people and injure 182.

25 November

Home Secretary, Roy Jenkins, introduces Prevention of Terrorism Act.

8 December

Irish Republican Socialist Party formed in Dublin.

10 December

Group of Protestant churchmen meet members of Provisional IRA and Provisional Sinn Fein at Feakle, Co Clare.

1975

16 January

Provisional IRA ends ceasefire begun on 20 December.

9 February

Provisional IRA declares indefinite ceasefire following talks with British officials.

11 February

Merlyn Rees announces establishment of 'incident centres' to monitor ceasefire.

16 February

Hunger strike by Provisional IRA prisoners in Portlaoise Prison ends; they are granted segregation from other prisoners.

25 February

Provisional Sinn Fein opens fourteen 'community centres' in Northern Ireland.

8 May

Northern Ireland Convention opens.

31 July

Three members of Miami Showband killed by UVF in Armagh.

15 August

Five people killed when Provisional IRA bombed Bayardo bar on Belfast's Shankill Road.

2 September

Six protestants shot dead at Tullyvallen Orange Hall in South Armagh by Provisional IRA using cover name 'Republican Action Force'.

2 October

Twelve people killed and forty-six injured in series of attacks by UVF.

3 October

UVF declared an illegal organization.

4 November

Merlyn Rees announces that 'special-category' status for prisoners will be phased out.

12 November

Merlyn Rees announces closure of Republican 'incident centres'.

5 December:

Internment without trial ends with release of last detainees.

1976

4 January

Five Catholics shot dead in two attacks by 'Protestant Action Force'.

5 January

Ten Protestant workers taken off bus at Kingsmills in Co Armagh and machine-gunned to death by Provisional IRA.

12 February

Republican Frank Stagg dies after sixty days on hunger strike in Wakefield Prison. Wave of shootings and bombings in Northern Ireland.

1 March

Persons committing terrorist offences no longer entitled to special-category status.

9 March

Northern Ireland Convention dissolved.

10 March

Former UDA Chairman Sammy Smyth shot dead.

10 March

Government of Irish Republic refers torture of internees case to European Court of Human Rights.

5 April

James Callaghan succeeds Harold Wilson as British Prime Minister.

11 April

Historian A. J. P. Taylor calls for speedy British withdrawal from Northern Ireland.

21 July

British Ambassador to Irish Republic, Christopher Ewart-Biggs, assassinated by Provisional IRA in landmine explosion under his car.

10 August

Three young Maguire children killed when Provisional IRA car driver shot dead by British troops in Belfast.

12 August

In response to the children's death, Betty Williams and Mairead Corrigan form 'Women's Peace Movement' later called 'The Peace People'.

21 August

20,000 people attend first Belfast Peace Rally.

28 August

30,000 Catholic and Protestant women march along Shankill Road for a rally in heart of Protestant Belfast.

2 September

European Commission on Human Rights finds Britain guilty of torture of internees in 1971.

4 September

More than 20,000 people attend Derry Peace Rally.

10 September

Roy Mason appointed Secretary of State for Northern Ireland.

28 October

Provisional Sinn Fein vice-president, Maire Drumm, shot dead in Mater Hospital, Belfast.

1977

23 January

Official Sinn Fein Ard Fheis change name to Sinn Fein the Workers' Party.

3 May

First day of Loyalist strike. Reports of widespread intimidation.

13 May

Loyalist strike called off.

29 May

UVF declares ceasefire and calls on other groups to do likewise.

9–10 August

Queen's Silver Jubilee visit to Northern Ireland.

28 September

Anglo-Irish summit in London between James Callaghan and Jack Lynch.

10 October

1976 Nobel Peace Prize awarded to Betty Williams and Mairead Corrigan.

1978

18 January

Britain found not guilty of torture by European Court of Human Rights, but guilty of 'inhuman degrading treatment'.

17 February

Twelve people killed and twenty-three injured when La Mon Restaurant in Co Down is destroyed by Provisional IRA fire-bombs.

1979

30 March

Irish National Liberation Army (INLA) bomb kills Airey Neave, Conservative spokesman on Northern Ireland, in House of Commons car park.

3 May

Conservatives win British General Election.

5 May

Humphrey Atkins appointed Secretary of State for Northern Ireland.

27 August

Provisional IRA bomb kills Lord Mountbatten of Burma in Mullaghmore Harbour, Co Sligo.

27 August

Provisional IRA kill eighteen British soldiers near Warrenpoint close to border with Irish Republic.

5 September

Prime Minister, Margaret Thatcher, holds Anglo-Irish summit with Jack Lynch, after Mountbatten funeral in Westminster Abbey.

29 September–1 October

Pastoral visit of Pope John Paul II to Ireland:

'To all men and women engaged in violence. I appeal to you. On my knees I beg you to turn away from the paths of violence and return to the ways of peace.

'I come to Drogheda today on a great mission of peace and reconciliation. I come as a pilgrim of peace, Christ's peace. To Catholics and Protestants, my message is peace and love. May no Irish Protestant think that the Pope is an enemy, a danger or a threat. My desire is that instead Protestants would see in me a friend and a brother in Christ.'

2 October

Provisional IRA reject Pope's appeal for an end to violence.

5 December

Jack Lynch announces his retirement as Prime Minister of Irish Republic. Succeeded by Charles Haughey.

1980

21 May

Anglo-Irish summit between Margaret Thatcher and Charles Haughey in London.

2 July

Humphrey Atkins announces Government proposals for a Northern Ireland Assembly of eighty elected members in place of direct rule from Westminster.

27 October

Seven Provisional IRA prisoners in H-Blocks of Maze Prison go on hunger strike in support of their demand to be treated as political prisoners.

8 December

Anglo-Irish summit between Margaret Thatcher and Charles Haughey in Dublin Castle.

19 December

Dirty Protest by 466 men in H-Blocks of Maze Prison called off after four-year campaign for political status.

1981

6 February

Journalists taken to see parade of 500 Loyalists in Antrim hills; according to Ian Paisley, all hold legal firearms certificates and are prepared to take action to prevent any union of Northern Ireland with Irish Republic.

1 March

Hunger strike begins in Maze Prison.

9 April

Provisional IRA hunger striker Bobby Sands wins Fermanagh and South Tyrone by-election.

28 April

Pope's personal envoy, John Magee, sees Bobby Sands and three other hunger strikers in Maze Prison.

5 May

Death of Bobby Sands in Maze Prison on sixty-sixth day of hunger strike.

30 June

Dr Garret FitzGerald elected Prime Minister of Irish Republic at head of Fine Gael and Labour coalition.

18 July

Thousands of hunger-strike supporters clash with police in Dublin as they try to demonstrate outside British Embassy.

31 July

Mother of hunger striker Patrick Quinn, on forty-seventh day of his fast, authorizes doctors to try to save his life.

20 August

Death of Michael Devine, tenth hunger striker to die in Maze Prison.

20 August

H-Block candidate Owen Carron wins Fermanagh and South Tyrone by-election.

14 September

James Prior appointed Secretary of State for Northern Ireland.

26 September

Liam McCloskey, INLA hunger striker, calls off his fast after fifty-five days because of intervention by his mother.

3 October

Hunger-strike campaign at Maze Prison called off.

6 October

James Prior announces details of prison reforms.

26 October

Bomb disposal expert killed while trying to defuse bomb in Oxford Street, London. Responsibility claimed by Provisional IRA.

6 November

Anglo-Irish summit in London between Margaret Thatcher and Dr Garret FitzGerald.

23 November

A 'Day of Action' staged in Northern Ireland by Ian Paisley to show dissatisfaction with Government's strategy against Provisional IRA.

1982
9 March

Charles Haughey elected Prime Minister of Irish Republic.

2 April

Argentina invades Falkand Islands.

5 April

James Prior introduces White Paper outlining Government's proposals for seventy-eight-member Northern Ireland Assembly.

4 May

Irish government announces it is opting out of EEC sanctions against Argentina.

20 July

Two soldiers killed by remote-control car bomb in Hyde Park. Six bandsmen killed by bomb placed under bandstand in Regent's Park. Responsibility claimed by Provisional IRA.

20 October

Northern Ireland Assembly elections.

21 October

James Prior announces that De Lorean sports car plant in Belfast – given about £80 million in government aid – is to close.

29 October

First meeting of 'Soldiers of the Cross' fellowship, for ex-paramilitaries who become Christians, held in Belfast.

11 November

Northern Ireland Assembly opens – boycotted by SDLP and Sinn Fein members.

6 December

Seventeen killed and sixty-six injured by bomb attack on Droppin Well Inn at Ballykelly. Responsibility claimed by Irish National Liberation Army.

14 December

Dr Garret FitzGerald elected Prime Minister of Irish Republic at head of Fine Gael and Labour coalition.

1983

11 April

At Belfast Crown Court, fourteen Loyalist terrorists jailed for total of more than 200 years on evidence of 'supergrass'.

30 May

New Ireland Forum opens in Dublin Castle – Fianna Fail, Fine Gael, Labour Party and SDLP take part.

9 June

Conservatives win British General Election. In Northern Ireland: SDLP 137,012 votes, Sinn Fein 102,681 votes.

3 July

Belfast home of Gerry Fitt, former MP for West Belfast, gutted by fire started by Provisional IRA.

25 September

Thirty-eight Republican prisoners escape from the Maze high-security prison near Belfast. One prison warder killed and several others injured.

7 November

Anglo-Irish summit at Chequers between Margaret Thatcher and Dr Garret FitzGerald.

20 November

Three church elders, Harold Brown, Victor Cunningham and David Wilson killed by gunmen at Mountain Lodge Pentecostal church near Darkley during Sunday evening worship. Alleged that Irish National Liberation Army gunmen carried out the attack.

17 December

Car-bomb placed outside Harrods in London kills six and injures ninety. Responsibilities claimed by Provisional IRA.

1984

9 February

Delegation representing Catholic Bishops of Ireland answer questions at New Ireland Forum.

17 March

Alleged INLA leader, Dominic McGlinchey, arrested in Irish Republic and later the same day extradited to Northern Ireland.

8 April

Mary Travers, daughter of Northern Ireland magistrate Thomas Travers, shot dead by Provisional IRA gunmen while walking home from church.

2 May

Publication of Report of New Ireland Forum. 'The particular structure of political unity which the Forum would wish to see established is a unitary state, achieved by agreement and consent, embracing the whole island of Ireland.'

17 May

Jim Campell, northern editor of Sunday World, shot and seriously wounded in Belfast after articles attacking paramilitaries. First journalist to be attacked during present troubles.

18 May

Two British soldiers killed and eleven people injured in car-bomb explosion in Enniskillen, Co Fermanagh. Two RUC men killed and a third seriously injured in landmine explosion near Camlough in South Armagh. Responsibility for both attacks claimed by Provisional IRA.

1–4 June

Visit to Ireland by President Ronald Reagan.

4 June

'The position of the United States is clear: We must not and will not interfere in Irish matters.' Address by President to joint session of Irish Parliament in Dublin.

14 June

Election to European Parliament. SDLP 183, 256 votes, Sinn Fein 93,079 votes, Ian Paisley's DUP 230,251 votes.

2 July
British House of Commons debate New Ireland Forum report.
12 August
One man killed by a plastic bullet fired by police and more than twenty injured as RUC attempt to arrest Martin Galvin, a Noraid leader, during an anti-internment commemoration in West Belfast. (Galvin was subjected to an exclusion order banning him from entering Northern Ireland.)
14 August
James Prior, Secretary of State for Northern Ireland, described the incident as 'an enormous setback' for himself and for the RUC. 'Some mistakes have been made, for which I take full responsibility myself.'